What People Are Saying

Sabrina

This is a deeply personal invocation of the natural history, mythology, and Spirit of Britain's greatest river, with a strong strain of practical magic. It is exciting, absorbing and endearing.
Professor Ronald Hutton, historian and author of *The Triumph of the Moon*, *The Stations of the Sun* and *Queens of the Wild*

By pulling on the threads woven across myth, lore, poetry, history, and literature, Brett Hollyhead has painted a glorious image of the Goddess Sabrina rooted within her own complex cultural context. A Goddess of the in-between, with a history and lore as convoluted and contradictory as her waters are deep and mysterious. And yet, this book has managed to explore these themes in an accessible and enchanting format. Brett has guided the reader on an epic adventure along the flow of the Severn, where they will learn of a Goddess who was perhaps born of a giant's tears or began her life as a poor drowned soul. Packed also with hands on practical exercises for the aspiring devotee or magical practitioner. All who read this will feel a deeper connection not only to the Goddess Sabrina, but also to the adjacent lore found within the cultures of the various peoples who live along the Severn's banks and beyond. A beautiful, poetic, and well-researched read. This book is a treasure, a gift that I'm certain many will find useful for many moons to come.
Mhara, Starling, author of *Welsh Witchcraft: A Guide to the Spirits, Lore, and Magic of Wales*

I encourage everyone to take Brett's hand and dip into the waters of the Severn with him as he guides you along the beautiful winding journey the river takes. It will lead you to one of the most fascinating goddesses, the elusive but alluring water nymph Sabrina. The book honours Sabrina in the most charming and wonderful way, you won't be disappointed.

Rachel Patterson, Witch and bestselling author of thirty books including *Gods & Goddesses of England, The Triple Goddess* and *The Cailleach.*

A wonderful and much-needed exploration of the myths and magic of the Severn, one of Britain's greatest rivers, and the goddess which bears its name. Delving into the history and lore of Sabrina, the author suggests some practical methods of working with this neglected deity and her region. Invaluable.

Liz Williams, lecturer and author of *Miracles of Our Own Making: A History of Paganism*

Pagan Portals - Sabrina is a fascinating look at not only Sabrina, the powerful figure connected to the river Severn, but of the stories written in the landscape and the endless cycles of the river. Blending history and myth with personal experience through a poetic writing style, this book speaks to the soul as much as to the mind, educating and enchanting. A must read for anyone interested in river goddesses or anyone drawn to the magic of water.

Morgan Daimler, author of *The Morrigan* and *Brigid*

Pagan Portals

Sabrina

Discovering the Goddess
of the River Severn

Pagan Portals

Sabrina

Discovering the Goddess
of the River Severn

Brett Hollyhead

The Witch of Salopia

MOON
BOOKS

London, UK
Washington, DC, USA

CollectiveInk

First published by Moon Books, 2025
Moon Books is an imprint of Collective Ink Ltd.,
Unit 11, Shepperton House, 89 Shepperton Road, London, N1 3DF
office@collectiveinkbooks.com
www.collectiveinkbooks.com
www.moon-books.net

For distributor details and how to order please visit the 'Ordering' section on our website.

Text copyright:Brett Hollyhead 2024

ISBN: 978 1 80341 807 0
978 1 80341 938 1 (ebook)
Library of Congress Control Number: 2024944156

A CIP catalogue record for this book is available from the British Library.

Design: Lapiz Digital Services

UK: Printed and bound by CPI Group (UK) Ltd, Croydon, CR0 4YY
US: Printed and bound by Thomson-Shore, 7300 West Joy Road, Dexter, MI 48130

We operate a distinctive and ethical publishing philosophy in
all areas of our business, from our global network of authors to
production and worldwide distribution.

Contents

To the great Goddess herself who's river I had the privilege of growing up next to. *Diolch o galon* for always watching over me and for imbuing me with your wisdom and inspiration in the process. Forever and always, this book is dedicated to you *Sabrina, Duwies yr afon, mam y gororau.*

To my beautiful partner, Moss Matthey, *mein herz gehört dir.*

And lastly this book is dedicated to *Cylch y Sarffes Goch,* for your infinite guidance and for making life more magical by the day. *Llawer o gariad i gyd.*

Acknowledgements

This book could not have come into existence without the guidance, patience and support of each wonderful individual who accompanied me upon this journey. I am indebted to each one of you and from the bottom of my heart I am truly grateful. First and foremost, I want to thank my partner Moss Matthey for encouraging me every step of the way and for being my rock. I don't know how you have put up with my restless emotions but your passion, your ability to listen and to inspire creativity within me is nothing short of a blessing. I am forever grateful to walk this path with you, to work magic side by side with you, and to be your fairy in all your TikTok videos. A special heartfelt thanks goes out to the rest of my coven; to Mhara Starling and Matthew Lewis for being the most fabulous witches I have ever encountered. Without you my path would never have taken the course it did; for it was your love of Wales that allowed me to uncover the hidden and overlooked magic of my home. Thank you for bringing me back to my roots and for all the nights spent giving me reassurance as I wept into my iced coffee. To all my friends and family for giving me the extra boost of confidence to pursue my dreams, I love you all eternally. I am also greatly appreciative of every single person who follows me on social media and to those who gave me the opportunity to have a platform to educate about the lore of the Welsh Marches. None of this could have been possible without you and I'm so deeply appreciative of your presence. To Trevor Greenfield for allowing me to publish with Moon books, I am so honoured to be a part of the team and I can't express my gratitude enough. And lastly a special thank goes out to the Chester pole fitness committee and Larissa Bishop, the most amazing captain for bringing me a touch of American glamour from the same place the Goddess Sabrina established herself.

Map of the River Severn

Introduction

There is a gentle Nymph not far from hence
That with moist curb sways the smooth Severn stream.[1]

Wild swimming has always held my heart. Whenever the need for the water calls, I am compelled to answer, plunging myself into the rhythmic tides of the River Dee in Llangollen. Time is erased, the pressures of society halted, and I am free to immerse myself in a beautiful, luminous realm where dragonflies dance upon the surface and the touch of the curious, over hanging willow trees brush my skin. Peace ensnares me.... that is until something slimy touches me and makes my soul want to leave my body.

For many, swimming is a past time or a way to get fit, but for me it is an escape, with every stroke a passage into the liminal where the stress of the everyday world cannot touch me. Here, in my regular swimming spot, my very sense of self dissolves into swirling waves of cosmic energy, connecting me to my wider surroundings and the aquatic source of life itself. Yet, while swimming across the river, enclosed by the watchful gaze of the Horseshoe Mountain pass of North Wales, I cannot help but feel a deep nostalgia for the River Severn. This waterscape is flooded with the innocence of my childhood memories and lies at the centre of my practice as a witch. Unknown to many, there resides within this serpentine river an immortalised deity who embodies the remnants of ancient Celtic, Roman, and Medieval belief, as well as fascinating stories of spiritual transformation.

This deity carries a variety of names, including Sabrina in English, and Hafren in Welsh, but her nature cannot be contained in any singular epithet. Goddess, God, Land spirit, Guardian, Virgin, Nymph, and Specter, Sabrina has embodied them all. Just like the element that forms her course, she can never be contained, for she is ineffable, constantly changing and flowing past restrictive dichotomies and labels, refusing to ever be truly categorised. However, she is perhaps best known today simply as Sabrina, and that is the name I will use to refer to her throughout these pages.

First Encounters

Originating from high up in the dark, marshy, Cambrian mountains of Wales, the River Severn is the longest river in Britain. Sabrina's waters travel for 220 miles, winding through the ancient towns and villages of the Welsh Marches. She begins her journey on the slopes of the Pumlumon mountain range, cascading down through Powys to Shropshire, Worcestershire, Gloucestershire and finally ending up in the Celtic Sea via the Bristol channel.

I was born next to Sabrina and grew up alongside, as she travels through my childhood homes. Both in Shropshire with my mother and in Wales with my father, I spent many happy summers submerging my feet in her cool, inviting waves. No matter how far I strayed, the Goddess would always call me home. When I was young, I would often visit the dingle, a sunken garden located in the middle of the hustle of Shrewsbury town life which sits adjacent. To me this was always more than simply a garden.

The dingle is a floral masterpiece bursting with colour and fragrance, enticing any who visit Shrewsbury to explore the beauty it holds; a sanctuary of flowers that I eagerly explored. My first visit is one I will never forget. Whilst running along its circling paths I was stopped in my tracks by the sudden appearance of an astonishing statue which I had never noticed before. In a rare moment of silence amongst all the excitement, I examined the statue before me; a beguiling woman of stone resting upon her side, lifting her hair, and gazing at her reflection in the pool surrounding her. Though she appeared calm and dignified, I was overcome with a feeling of sorrow that hung heavy in the air between us. I asked my mother who she was. This was the Goddess Sabrina, she told me, drowned at an early age, and forever bound to this river as its guardian. We had finally met in flesh and stone.

Riverine Creator

Before we delve any deeper into Sabrina's lore, it is helpful to take a moment to contemplate water. Throughout history, rivers have been venerated as the embodiment of the divine. Existing in the liminal state between the tangible and mythological, they have provided the heart of many practices and beliefs. Within them the forces of regeneration, revitalisation and destruction coalesce to form the essence of water's magic and potential. Sabrina's waters, as with many other river deities, have tended the ebb and flow of life, death, and rebirth since the beginning of time. Within both scientific discovery and sacred narratives across the world, the genesis of life is increasingly linked to the primordial waters from which we emerged. During the evolution of the earth, scientist's hypothesise complex molecular life began upon the ocean floor at hypothermal vents that initiated chemical synthesis to build the foundations of life.[2] These waters of creation can also be seen in the many cultural beliefs and mythologies of the celestial bodies arising from the depths of the aquatic domain.[3] This is often, but not exclusively, personified as a feminine figure who governs the gestation of the world, birthing it into existence just as humanity develops within the amniotic fluid of the womb.

Sabrina, like many other water deities, is polysemous by nature, meaning she embodies a wide range of differing and sometimes contradictory attributes all at the same time. She is healer, destroyer, protective, emotional and animalistic as well as ordered and peaceful. In addition, she is also often linked to the concept of the ancestral source. This is not simply an archetype that arises in the collective unconsciousness but refers to something deeper – an ancient presence that is the beginning and end, where all life comes from and must return.

Where there is water, there is the reminder that we are its children. Even our bodies are composed of around 60% water.[4] We seek its nourishment, its ability to cure and to clean, and our spirits yearn to be connected to its intimate presence. We are conceived in liquid, we leave this world through liquid as we decay, we bleed, we sweat, we cry and urinate as complex fluid bodies. When we approach a water source like the River Severn, feelings of peace seem to wash over us, unable to be captured by words, for water speaks the language of the heart. Sabrina is experiential. In each droplet we feel the Goddess, caught in her currents that remind us of our constant connection to her.

Rivers have even been described as the veins of the earth itself, depositing nutrients, and minerals to the wider ecosystem by mingling salt and freshwater.[5] While Sabrina is the embodiment of this parental instinct, creating a home for a variety of flowers and wildlife as well as acting as a boundary protectress, she is not without ambivalence. Rivers are depicted as life givers, but their roles are balanced by their ability to wreak devastation. The Welsh Marches has often been on the receiving end of her rage with Sabrina claiming many bodies of those unfortunate enough to have drowned in her waters; a constant reminder of her ability to bring death. But this does not mean that the Goddess should be feared, for she merely expresses the teachings reflected within all nature. There is always a balance. This is especially evident when her destructive forces have extended beyond her banks and flooded my homeland on countless occasions, yielding a greater crop in the year that follows. This balance gives any who wish to work with her extra reason to be respectful when engaging with her elemental teachings.

A Turbulent Past – A Hopeful Future

While water may often appear to be peaceful and calm, the history of the Goddess is far from an image of tranquillity. Sabrina has seen multiple epochs of brutality to which her waters still retain a collection of blood-stained memories. The land of the Goddess, referred to as the Welsh Marches, is a terrestrial and cultural hybrid forged between two nations whose interactions with each other were not often peaceful, going through various stages of warfare, conquest, and political fragility. To understand the disputes from each side of the river is to understand Sabrina herself, for her identity is tied to her dual affinity for the people of Celtic and Saxon heritage. Sabrina forges the intermediary bridge between the present and violent past, and to this day she continues to challenge the demarcation of borders and their arbitrary definitions of what it means to belong to a specific group. The Goddess herself beautifully expresses this paradox.

Many claim she is Celtic, and rightly so, for her source lies firmly in the heartland of dragons. Others claim she is English as she runs through the English countryside. Neither are incorrect, yet both are insufficient to capture her essence.

The Marches are the result of cross pollination of language, customs and traditions that have created a distinct landscape. Even today the so called "English" counties she runs through have always remained unique in their identity due to their proximity to the border and their once Welsh past; a past which was not properly incorporated into England until the 16th-17th century. Fluid exchange of control between England and Wales has, as a result, produced a land piece that will always remain independent and coherent in its Anglo-Welsh identity with Sabrina as its sovereign queen, the ruler of the in-between.

Sabrina's river also boasts of the second highest bore in the world. This is a striking, natural phenomena caused by the union of the River Severn estuary's narrow channels and the entrance of the rising tide which generates a surging wave reaching heights up to two meters. Onlookers observe both in awe and in terror with the bore reputed both as a perfect spot for surfers and a mass force of destruction, taking the lives of those who fall victim to its grasp. According to the 9th century Welsh monk Nennius, the River Severn bore formed part of the Wonders of Britain as Dai Ri Hafren, the Two kings of the River Severn.[6] Contained within the masses of foam, the two kings collide like battling rams over and over with each wave, combining the elemental powers of Sabrina's waters and representing the incompatible histories of their kingdoms as they contend for the river's affection.

However, Sabrina's River today faces more challenges, for she has been taken for granted in the modern age. To our ancestors, the river would have been ever-present, irrigating their crops and quenching their thirst. They could not have ignored its power even if they tried and if they did, they would know the consequences of mistreating water. Modernity has changed this immensely. Exploited, poisoned, polluted, and rendered as a dispensable commodity, the distance between us and the divinity within our rivers has been slowly increased by capitalism, industrialisation, and consumerism. But in the age of awareness towards our environment, the sanctity of water and our dependence upon it is being recognised and appreciated once more. We are being called home to the Goddess and to rejoice with her and all that she governs.

Regardless of our spiritual beliefs, when we approach the various waterscapes that meander through our everyday life, there is an ache of familiarity that is both inspiring and demanding of reverence. It is my hope that this book speaks to that ache through the magic and mythology of Sabrina. It explores her cultural connections and beliefs that have grown around her to help those who want to initiate a relationship with her or who simply want to learn a little more. This book is an introduction and a personal love letter to Sabrina, and by extension, to my home. Through its pages I will shed light on her stories, sharing with you a Goddess who has been with me my whole life and continues to guide me and many others. Sabrina is there for everyone who wishes to dive into her watery realm and explore her role in some of the most beautiful and important mythology in Paganism.

No matter where you are in the world, or whether there is a flowing water source nearby your home, her water connects all things. We are a part of her through the water in our blood and through the air we breathe. We are never separated no matter how many urban walls, skylines or buildings are built between us and the Goddess. Our spirits can always connect with her from the weather worn summits to the swirling sapphire magnificence of the ocean.

Chapter 1

Beloved Nymph

What exactly is Sabrina's origin story? Is she a river Goddess attested in ancient sources and archaeological evidence? Is she a relic of a lost oral tradition? Or is she perhaps a fanciful figure, invoked to personify the River Severn for entertainment? Unfortunately, as with many deities across Britain, Sabrina and her beginnings in ancient history remain obscure. Yet approaches towards uncovering the Goddess have often been reductionist, assuming the form we know her as today existed unchanged many years ago within ancient communities. But water continuously changes, flowing through the land as a representation of nature's impermanence. Her origins are complicated and contradictory, yet combined they give us a clear picture of the Riverine Goddess. Just like the River Severn contains multiple tributaries that flow into the river to give it form, so too does Sabrina contain many origins, names, and beliefs. Within my own practice, Sabrina is a deity that expands beyond one singular definition and encompasses a vast assembly of divine sources, stories, and customs that connect all people past and present to her waters.

Through an examination of etymology, literature, and cultural correspondences, I have attempted to reveal the corpus of lore that comprises Sabrina. It's important for me to note that this is not to prove the belief in the Goddess in antiquity but to reveal Sabrina's presence and the joy that comes to those who wish to forge a relationship with her today. The notion of divinity is complex especially since each one of us will have a unique perception and understanding through our own encounters. But these personal revelations we experience with the Gods captures their essence and allows us to form deep and meaningful connections with them, even when the foundations of their origins have been eroded by the river of time. For the Gods are meant to be felt; to be experienced with the heart and soul. To me, Sabrina is the ruler of the living body of water that is the River Severn, with autonomy and vibrant personality that shifts through the seasons. Like many others who grew up with her, I know all too well her temperament; one day providing nourishment and destroying it in fits of rage the next. I still don't know to this day how she didn't drown me as a little boy after all the times I secretly relieved myself in her waters while swimming. Since she has affection for infants, I'd like to think Sabrina forgives childhood naivety; a mistake that I wouldn't dare make as an adult.

The stories and myths attached to her throughout this book are not fabrications of the mind or irrational tales as modern society would have us believe. They are expressive narratives that form and enrich the world we live in by giving meaning and significance to the relationship we have with the Goddess.[1] Each one can be viewed as a sacred reality that informs values and community connections caught in Sabrina's story.[2] Although Sabrina's true origins cannot be put fully into words, her beauty, her influence, and her profound wisdom give meaning to the Welsh Marches and the history that is recorded here. As Kristoffer Hughes states '*The Gods act as skeletons that form the bare bones of tradition and mythology*'.[3] The people of Sabrina's landscape and their stories give her the body that allows her to walk among us in the modern day.

If we do look back at her history, her most popular story is littered with vindictiveness and violence, resulting in the drowning of the innocent. In 1136, the medieval cleric and chronographer Geoffrey of Monmouth, fashioned together the *History of the Kings of Britain*; a pseudohistorical piece that claimed to lay the foundation of British history and civilisation and which contains the first literary origin of Sabrina, where he referred to her as Habren.[4]

Geoffrey claimed to have translated his work into Latin from a mysterious book written in an "ancient British language", given to him by Walter, Archdeacon of Oxford. This was basically the medieval version of "trust me bro" when asked for his sources. No evidence has been found of this book's existence, leading many to believe that Geoffrey's sources of inspiration were derived from his predecessors.[5] This includes *On the Ruin of Britain* by Gildas in the 6th century, *The Ecclesiastical History of the English* by Bede in the 8th century and *The History of the Britons* by Nennius in the 9th century, as well as various additional texts and the medieval oral culture of Monmouth stitched together by his vivid imagination. Nevertheless, his composition of work paved the way for the subsequent literature about Sabrina.

The Drowned Daughter of Locrinus

Our story begins with Brutus, an exile of Troy and the first king of Britain, who, upon his death granted territory to his three sons and his second in command. Locrinus, the first-born son, was granted rulership of Lloegeria (England), Kamber ruled the land beyond the River Severn to the west known as Kymry (Wales), Albanactus took rulership of the northern lands of Albany (Scotland) and lastly, his second in command Corineus was gifted the kingdom of Cornwall. All seemed well under each ruler, until Albanactus was slain in battle by the invading Huns and their vicious leader, Humber. However, his death united Locrinus' and Cambers' kingdoms in opposition.

After they emerged victorious, Locrinus discovered three damsels held captive among the spoils of war. One of these was no ordinary prisoner but in fact a beautiful Germanic princess called Estrildis. She proved irresistible to Locrinus, and he fell head over heels in love the moment he saw her. As with all stories involving such beauty, the distraction and seduction of the king would be sure to bring about the ruin of his Kingdom. He could not contain his love for Estrildis and treated her as if she were his own wife. But there was one little problem. The king of England was already betrothed to Gwendolen, the daughter of Corineus. As soon as he received word of this betrayal, Corineus was enraged, and threatened Locrinus to honour his betrothal or else he would feel the sharp end of an axe.

Before the blow could be struck, Locrinus' men intervened and persuaded the King of England to honour his commitment to Gwendolen. Under the pretence of complying, the cunning king hid Estrildis in an underground chamber for seven years. This was said to be either by the River Thames in London or the River Severn in Caersws. Regardless of positioning, Locrinus made many journeys to see his beloved while claiming to be sequestered in prayer. Within the depths of the earth's embrace, he fathered a child: Habren. Estrildis' fruitfulness had provided an heir to the throne and thus she became a living part of the land, buried deep beneath the soil until her power came to fruition through her beautiful child.

Once Corineus had passed, Locrinus seized the opportunity to cast aside his old wife to be with Estrildis and his daughter. But Gwendolen would not go quietly. She was a great woman scorned and used her paternal connections to seek out vengeance to stop the usurping of the royal line by the bastard child. She summoned the men of Cornwall to declare war upon her husband, and the two armies met in battle at the banks of the River Stour near London. They fought until the last of King Locrinus' war cries were uttered in his dying breath.

However, Gwendolen was not content with the death of her unfaithful husband alone. To end her wrath, she commanded that both Estrildis and her daughter, Habren, be drowned in the River Severn. Some say the tragic event occurred in Dolforwyn, which to this day bears the name "maidens meadow", carrying forth the tragic notions of Gwendolen's merciless act. As an everlasting memorial to the youth, Gwendolen ensured the river bore her name as a symbol of her husband's unfaithfulness and infidelity. However, it is said the spirits of the river took pity on the poor child and with one kiss snatched Habren away from the grasp of death and transformed her into the immortal Goddess we know today.

Birth of the Goddess

Sabrina's tale does not end with her drowning, for the Goddess has an alternative origin, woven into the Welsh landscape itself. In this Celtic lore, Sabrina is untroubled by the undertakings of kings and instead concerns herself with the circulation of her waters through the hydrological cycle. It is uncertain where the tale originates, but it is features prominently through the works of Bill Gwilliam who gathered it from 17th century antiquary Thomas Habington. The story also features in John Rhys' works where he recollects the story from his childhood:

Tair afon gynt a rifwyd
Ar ddwyfron Pumlumon lwyd
Hafren a Gwy, hyfryd eu gwedd
A Rheidol, fawr ei anrhydedd

Three rivers of yore were seen
On grey Pumlumons breast
Severn and Wye of pleasant mien
And Rheidol rich in great renown[6]

Here, Sabrina is not born of mortal blood but birthed innumerable times, alongside her sisters, from the protective giant, Pumlumon. Giants feature prominently throughout Wales with various place names still carrying the memory of their ominous presence, especially near mountains. Pumlumon itself, is a distinctive area which forms the Cambrian Mountains alongside the Elenydd and Mynydd Mallaen. Pumlumon can be translated to mean "the five beacons", the tallest being Pumlumon Fawr which seems to touch the sky itself, forming a beautiful yet remote landscape, free from human disturbance beyond the occasional walker. It is here in the very heart of Wales, drenched with rain and filled with acidic soil and bogs that the birth of the Goddess occurs.

Sabrina, or Hafren to invoke her Welsh name within the story, is born alongside Wye, also referred to as Gwy or her Latin name Vaga, and Rheidol to restore vitality to the land. Rheidol is sometimes interchanged with Ystwyth depending on the adaptation of the tale with both rivers merging during the end of their course towards the seaside town of Aberystwyth. However, Poets have suggested that originally there were five water spirits with Llyffnant and Dulas[7]or alternatively Llyffnant and Mynach,[8] all of which make a vow to merge with the sea. No one knows why the other rivers were omitted; perhaps to reflect the importance of triplicity within the Celtic continuum. Regardless of the exact reasons, Sabrina's story is passed down to us as follows.

Tears of a Giant

High up in the Mountains of Powys, the mighty giant, Pumlumon, a formidable entity who contained the power of creation, cried three tears out of loneliness and frustration for the sight of the desolate lands that surrounded him. From these tears grew three strong and enchanting nymphs, nurtured under the protection of their father. Pumlumon loved these nymphs dearly and named them Rheidol, Hafren and Gwy.

With each passing day the nymphs grew stronger and more beautiful, but they could not quite surpass their yearning for the wild currents of the Celtic Sea. Understanding this desire Pumlumon embraced them and sent them along their way with his blessing. Rheidol, the first daughter rushed as quickly as possible, dancing her way merrily through Wales towards Aberystwyth to re-join with the sea as the first among her sisters. On the other hand, Gwy, the Youngest of the three nymphs, took her time visiting the sights of the land, bringing tranquillity with every step she took, meandering through the moorlands towards Chepstow before eventually reaching the sea. Finally, Hafren, the fairest of them all, with her father's blessings pursued her urge for knowledge and culture; taking the longest route through the countryside and the human kingdoms to learn their ways. The young nymph brought enchantment to the people who embraced her and floods to those who dared to take advantage of her kind nature. Eventually all three sisters converged in harmony and fulfilment together, discussing all that they had learned and seen along their travels.

Their father was not saddened by their departure for he knew that his daughters would soon return to him. Through the hydrological cycle, the three sisters ride gracefully upon the clouds to return to their father in the form of rain, with each elegant droplet carrying the power of potential and creation. Once rejoined the ethereal nymphs are reborn to continually flow from Pumlumon along their originally forged paths as the aquatic overseers of all life.

Sabrina's Lessons

We learn much from both these tales of Sabrina. As humans, we need stories. They provide a way for us to learn valuable moral lessons, the secrets to happiness and allow a glimpse into all aspects of the human condition, granting us deep knowledge of ourselves. For anyone seeking to know the Goddess, Sabrina's stories pave the foundations for forming relationships with her and give testament to how she has infatuated the imagination of the people and the land. Her drastically different origin points, where our empathy bleeds for the innocent and our admiration soars for the gift of liquid precipitation, might seem, at first, incompatible. But they are not irreconcilable as they teach of the multifaceted nature of the Goddess, imparting important lessons from both the corporeal and transcendent realm. Geoffrey's tale represents the dangers of political and geographical alliances and how the unrestrained, lustful individuals in power often make life unbearable for those caught in the crossfire, a lesson that still rings true today.

Sabrina's demise precedes her transformation into the Goddess, a stunning example of apotheosis, and a testament to her divine power in the face of such misfortune. We see a glimpse of the mythological conflict that has shaped her lands, an essential aspect to understanding Sabrina. And we learn of the power of water to transcend fate, taking a powerless drowned youth and transforming her into a nymph who is adored to this day.

Her Welsh origins are equally potent. The lore of the wild, blithe, water spirit reveals to us the mysteries and connective force of water. She finds the course of least resistance, leaving her father to distribute beauty to Wales and the Welsh Marches before she traverses through to the sea. When it rains upon our brow, each droplet is a reminder that Sabrina is ever present and that we are never alone. Learning these tales as a child opened my eyes to the wonder of Sabrina and how she plays such a vital role on a wider scale.

Ultimately, our first encounters with the Goddess are through myth and narrative. We learn much about her from these sources and knowing a little more about her we can now greet her as we would an old friend. But there is far more to be discovered just below the surface.

Chapter 2

A Historical Goddess

Pursuing Sabrina's descent through the mists of time is a path littered with speculation and impediment. From my own exploration of historical and academic sources, I have likened this to the yellow brick road from the *Wizard of Oz*. Each step an encounter with wonder and intrigue, confusion, and occasional hopelessness until I reach my destination; only to be told by the academics or collectively the "Wizard" to go away and come back tomorrow. An endless cycle, back and forth until I realised home was with me all along...there's no place like Sabrina.

What I essentially mean by this is those seeking an intimate connection with the Goddess of the River Severn must always remember to keep one foot firmly planted into the modern day, especially when exploring or reconstructing the beliefs of the past. There are no ancient temples to Sabrina or shrines dedicated in her honour, nor are there cults, inscribed objects, offerings, or written material before the 12th century. Even the Romans first described the River Severn as a strategic site for fortification rather than an otherworldly Goddess.

Yet excavation and scholarly rigor have provided some rich sources to illuminate the mysteries contained within the River Severn's transmutable nature. They provide us a window to glimpse the early beginnings of the Goddess and how our ancestors might have honoured her. But it is our own personal gnosis which maintains her current, symbolic importance. A lack of an agreed consensus as to whether Sabrina was an ancient Goddess or not does not dispute her modern divine presence.

Sabrina is deeply lodged within the Welsh Marches, blossoming with each rising tide, and adorned with the stories of the people in connection with her. Simply sitting along her banks, you can't help but feel the pure bliss that is her body; holding space for so many species to thrive within her. This is worthy of awe and veneration, activated by the process of apotheosis; the divine elevation of Sabrina to a status that may have not been ascribed to her in time long gone, but certainly is now due to her power to inspire. This is the cry of the Goddess, through each modern statue carved in her honour: *"I am here and you are here with me, in this space, in this time, in this experience."*

I am not an archaeologist or historian. When I'm down on my hands and knees it is very often for the purpose of cursing my ex in the woods or gathering certain plants for my spell work rather than digging for the past. But while exploring the history of the Goddess for this chapter I can't help but notice we are not entirely abandoned by evidence, especially when we investigate her name and importance of the River Severn to ancient populations.

What's in a Name?

The first place to discover Sabrina's origin is within the variety of names that have been given to her. The people who approached her used specific names for a reason, and we know names are incredibly important in Celtic culture. Much ink has been spilled tracing the etymologies of our favourite Gods and heroes. We learn much from their chosen titles when we examine them closely; Sabrina is no exception to this.

The River Severn is one of the oldest named rivers in Britain. Her divine being was first recorded in the 2nd century as a prominent feature of various Celtic tribal territories thanks to Ptolemy.[1] Claudius Ptolemy was an ancient Greek mathematician and astronomer who, through his works such as the *Geographica Hyphegesis*, documented Britain under the rulership of the Roman Empire. Here we see the beloved river named in Latin as Sabrina Fluvius.[2] This epithet was further featured within the

Annals by Roman historian and senator Tacitus, who recorded her name as Sabrinam.[3] Sadly, we don't truly know what Sabrina meant to them or whether the Romans took a preexisting name in the early Brythonic language. However, her name today is used interchangeably to refer to both the Goddess and river with Severn being a later anglicisation of the Latin Sabrina.

Before undergoing grammatical transformation, the name Severn first appeared in the *Anglo-Saxon Chronicles* as Sæfern[4] which may have derived from the old English word for sea, appearing in other words such as Sæbât (Sea-boat) and Sæfisc (Sea-fish).[5] Alternatively, the name could have originated from the rush plant which is referred to as Seave in some regional British dialects with the River Severn spelt as Seavern in the 13th century.[6] The rush plant natively grows along the banks of the River Severn and was commonly used by various Anglo-Saxon inhabitants to construct baskets to catch fish. However, the River Severn also had an alternative name that carried negative connotations in the old English language, referencing the terrible fate that befell the Saxons in Britain after their arrival and pursuit of the Britons over the river.

In 577, the Saxon leader Ceawlin of Wessex triumphed over the native Britons at Dyrham, Gloucestershire causing them to flee across the River Severn. However, when the Saxon warriors tried to pursue them, they met a watery grave. Sabrina and her many currents and whirlpools reclaimed their souls to the depths. This act earned her the additional name Unla; meaning misfortune.[7] We begin to see Sabrina emerge as a protectress, existing in the past as the defender of the Celts and acting as their boundary by thwarting the attempts of various invaders from crossing over.

These names are not necessarily indicative of divinity but looking to Sabrina's Welsh name, Hafren, we see her consciousness emerge within the poetic language of the Celts, manifesting as a being of the wilderness and the passage of time. Hafren is generally interpreted to mean summer flow,[8] the season that replenishes the earth with vitality. This developed from the old Welsh name Habren, Habrena or Hafriain meaning queen of Summer[9] which in turn came from the old Brythonic Sabren/Sabre before the S consonant was dropped for the H in the development of the Welsh language.[10] This is possibly where the Romans adopted the name, but scholars have reason to believe that the name Sabrina was already in their arsenal due to it being attached to a different river in Armenia during the Roman Empire.[11] However, in Welsh, Hafnai, a word very close to Hafren, can also be used as an insult to describe a disreputable woman. Therefore, its possible Hafren may be a tongue and cheek name given to the Goddess for betraying her homeland of Wales to flow into England to mix with the enemy.[12] Further research suggests that Sabrina's name derives from Samarosina to mean land of the summer time fallow but this may not be the case especially when other writers have broken down her name to the hypothetical Sa(m)-beru-ina supposedly meaning she of waters foaming together[13] which does not connect in any way, shape, or form to the term Samarosina.

Interestingly some have attempted to connect Sabrina with Hindu mythology. This may seem a little far-fetched due to geographical distance between Wales and India, but the modern languages spoken in these two countries has been hypothesised to originate from a common ancestor. In Hindu belief, Varuna is the celestial God of the oceans, and this name could have possibly been the root word for Sabrina, thus reinforcing a watery connection.[14] The Sanskrit word Sab is also interpreted to mean milk[15] which reveals a creatrix aspect to the Goddess who imbues the land with her maternal flowing waters.

I have spent many nights pulling my hair out and chugging coffee into the early hours of the morning trying to decipher her original name, but to no avail. The currents of time have dragged it below the surface, giving only tantalising glimpses of maybes and possibilities. However, we can learn powerful lessons from all the names she carries, as they have stood the test of time, speaking of her prismatic nature.

Sacred Deposits

Sabrina's divinity could potentially be evidenced by riverine deposits made by the Neolithic, Bronze age and Iron age communities of Britain. Prehistoric people often settled near rivers as they provided natural sources of trade, transportation, and irrigation[16] as well as a numinous meeting place to commune with spirits or to enact out ceremonial rites.[17] Multiple items including jewellery and weaponry have been pulled from Britain's rivers; intentionally and irretrievably cast into the depths until the revolutions of modern-day technology uncovered them. Ronald Hutton, professor, historian, and leading authority on the Pagan history of Britain speculates these activities could have a variety of meanings including the propitiation of river spirits and deities.[18] With the people exposed to the merciless elements, acts of veneration such as the deposition of objects into the river could potentially appease the deity and stave off their destructive capabilities. Weaponry has often been found purposefully damaged before being given to the river so that no human hands may wield them again. This may be interpreted as a consecrated act of protection with rivers forming territorial boundaries that could have been strengthened with items associated with war and defence.[19]

Sabrina's river, however, has a different story to tell compared to the exceeding number of objects uncovered in other notable rivers such as the Thames. Despite the River Severn's size, very little has been found due to restrictive environmental factors as well as differences in social cohesion between the westbound communities of what is Wales and the Welsh Marches.[20] In 2012, Mullin recorded 13 Bronze age items such as swords and axes from within the River Severn with a higher preference of deposition found in the silent and otherworldly terrain of wetlands and bogs. This doesn't exclude the idea of Sabrina being venerated from within the River Severn, but it does indicate that the river was not necessarily a boundary in need of weaponry to increase its protective virtue, but a place of unity and fluid crossing for the local tribes. Despite this, Sabrina's river reminisces over a time marked by the appearance of complex Neolithic structures. These include ring ditches, timber circles and henges and those later built from stone which all bore significance to the generations that constructed them. Not too far from where I lived were various henges including Sarn-y-bryn-caled and Dyffryn Lane Henge which may have marked strategic points for exchange and for ceremonial use. These were in close proximity to the River Severn which may have served to heighten the phenomena occurring inside.[21]

Early inhabitants, specifically the Iron age people stemming between 800BCE and 43CE, are often titled Celts. This term has driven years of debate and speculation but is now commonly used as a linguistic term to denote similarities in language and culture within a kaleidoscope of territories across Asia Minor, Europe, Britain and Ireland.[22] The Celts were not a unified group based on migration or invasion, but their Celticity arose from the trading of beliefs, material culture and language via the Atlantic trading routes.[23] Across the River Severn, many Celtic tribes settled, referred to as Insular Celts or Brythons whose language preceded the modern Celtic languages of Welsh, Cornish and Bretton. These included:

- Cornovii – Northeast Wales, Shropshire, Cheshire, and parts of Staffordshire
- Ordovices – Central and east Wales
- Dobunni – Herefordshire, Worcestershire, Gloucestershire, and Somerset
- Silures – South Wales

Their religious beliefs were expressed through the veneration of the natural world with trees, rivers and other geographical features deified and equipped with distinct functions. These were worshipped by the local tribes in sacred spaces known as groves and potentially during seasonal ceremonies upon the hillforts constructed at the time.[24] It is possible the tribes of the River Severn would have venerated the river as the source of their survival, knowing its power to bring about successful crop production as well as devastation. However, due to the changing landscape through time, no grove has been uncovered, nor any written evidence or mythology for us to deduce the extent of their beliefs before the Roman invasion in 43CE. Whatever beliefs these people had now take refuge in the silent memories of the standing stones across the river's course. One includes the single stone known as Carreg Wen which stands near Sabrina's source alongside the burial tombs of Pumlumon's earliest inhabitants.

Mother Goddess

Stephen J Yeates, archaeologist and author of *The Tribe of Witches*[25] suggested the worship of Sabrina was integral to the Dobunni. He identified several sites where ritualistic behaviour occurred including the offering of various objects at Lincombe and Holt as well as the Aust cliff. This once homed an Iron Age-Roman temple that overlooked the River Severn Estuary and all those who voyaged across.[26] Here a bronze statuette was discovered on the banks of the river where it may have fallen, depicting a feminine figure adorned with the moon upon her head; a potential lunar deity associated with the ebb and flow of the River Severn's waters.[27] Yeates also identified another sculpture uncovered from the remains of a ruined temple under what is now Saint Mary de Lodes Church. This sculpture was believed to be the Roman Goddess, Fortuna, who Yeates believed stood in as a substitute for various water Goddesses.[28]

Sabrina as a Goddess, therefore, may have been assimilated into the image of other deities allowing for the continuation of her divinity without it being explicitly stated. This was further purported by Yeates who believed Sabrina, alongside other deities in the same vicinity such as Cuda, Rosmerta and depictions of mother figures imported from Gaul, collectively known as "Matres" were indicative of a cult dedicated to a great mother. This was known as Mater Dobunna, a divine being heavily associated with sacred vessels. Her survival was rooted within the topography of the River Severn valley which was believed to be bowl or cauldron shaped in the same way as the sacred vessels were in the depictions of the tribal Goddesses. This may have inspired the name of the Dobunni and the Saxon Hwicce who later occupied the territory and potentially shared the same beliefs. However, Yeates' theories have since been proven inaccurate and difficult to verify. Considering the animistic beliefs of the Celts and what little evidence we do have; it would be very surprising if the River Severn was not venerated in some form.

Interpretatio Romana

Sabrina's river provided the impeccable location for the Romans to establish their legionary forts during their invasion of Britain under the reign of Emperor Claudius. Many of my school trips were spent visiting them including the famous Viroconium Cornoviorum which prospered to become the 4th largest Roman settlement after the Celtic tribes of the region were subdued. I can only cringe at the thought of the Cornovii Spirits looking down at me with a raised eyebrow whilst me and my school friends adorned ourselves in Roman armour replicas.

But where the Celtic expression of divinity remained largely silent, the Roman occupation birthed their image through iconographical depictions, inscriptions and architecture built in honour of the Gods with recognisable human faces.[29]

In the past, examination of the Celtic-Romano period has been interpreted through the process of Romanisation. Overpowered, the conquered tribes were forced to endure the fracturing of identity and belief while integrated into Roman culture,[30] especially via Interpretatio Romana. This is the process whereby the Celtic Gods were conceptualised through the Roman Pantheon, especially through the pairing of names.

However, Romanisation has since been proven inadequate in exploring the complex phenomena during this time and, contrary to popular thought, the Romans encouraged the continuation of the Celtic religion. Perceptions of deity and cultural blending was particularly affected by an individual's social class.[31] Jane Webster further supported this, identifying different categories of deities that developed beyond those with paired names.[32] This includes deities that emerged from the counterculture that were neither native or Roman but formed a hybrid pantheon, as well as those that may have arisen out of a need to explain a new phenomenon and therefore given a Celtic sounding name.[33] Perhaps this is what happened with Sabrina. Alternatively, her divinity may have been bound in the Roman belief in nymphs which infiltrated the empire via ancient Greece.

Although a semi divine entity, nymphs served an important function as both the guardians of vital aspects of nature, such as water deposits as well as embodiments of fertility, desire, and liberation.[34] In 1984 a Roman Temple in Littledean was discovered within the bend of the River Severn which was argued by Dr Anne Ross to be a nymphaeum or cult shrine to the Goddess Sabrina, with various artifacts uncovered including sandstone figurines, stone heads and objects depicted with images of salmon.[35] Links to the Goddess are still speculative due to no inscriptions bearing her name. It seems attempts at unearthing Sabrina's time-honoured residence within the River Severn's locale have been conjecture at best, but the many pieces do start to add up. However, there is one place that has provided favourable insight into the river's veneration: this time in the form of a masculine presenting deity.

God of the Raging Bore

In the 1920s a 3rd–4th century Roman temple that was built upon a previous Iron age Hillfort was discovered within Lydney Park, Gloucestershire, positioned to overlook the River Severn estuary. But rather than being dedicated to the Goddess this was instead dedicated to the Celtic-Romano God, Nodens. Various cult objects, inscriptions and images of aquatic life on the temple's mosaics have been found testifying to the power of this maritime deity and his associations with healing, dreams, hunting, fishing, and the bore.[36] No statues have been found of Nodens but we have a clear image of how he would have been perceived with the discovery of a bronze ceremonial headdress, depicting him riding on a chariot pulled by horses while carrying a sceptre and surrounded by winged entities as well as creatures that appear to be half centaur half fish.

Nodens is often conflated with several Roman deities including Mars and Silvanus to whom many people gave offerings of coins, pins, statues and letters to invoke his power in the fulfilment of certain actions including healing and cursing. A famous example of this comes from a lead cursing tablet directed at a Roman Citizen which reads:

To the God Nodens:
Silvianus has lost his ring
And given half (Its value) to
Nodens. Among those who are called Senicianus do
Not allow health until he
Brings it to the temple of
Nodens
(This Curse) comes into force again[37]

No doubt poor Senicianus probably had a rough time after this curse had been initiated. Primarily, Nodens operated within the depths of the liminal space between the waking world and the Otherworld by restoring the health of those who sought healing through sleep at his temple. This was believed to have been constructed as a dormitory to facilitate the incubation of visionary experiences through dreams which were later interpreted for healing insight.[38] Interestingly, statuettes of dogs have also been uncovered as an offering due to being associated with Nodens either as his representatives upon the spiritual plane who guide the afflicted, or as personal healers kept at the temple for their curative saliva.[39] His name also radiates with an otherworldly presence as it was deciphered by no other than the creator of the lord of the rings, J. R. R. Tolkien, who defined Nodens as catcher or hunter.[40] Nodens later mutated to the Welsh form of Nudd, to mean mist or haze, which is cognate to several characters in Welsh and Irish literature. Examples include the Irish Nuada Airgetlàm or Nuada of the silver hand and the Welsh King Lludd Llaw Eraint[41] (Lludd of the silver hand.) Nudd is also found related to famous characters in Welsh mythology such as the king of the Otherworld, Gwyn ap Nudd, who is heavily associated with hunting and otherworldly dogs.

It then begs the question whether Sabrina was originally perceived as a masculine God and preserved indirectly through later medieval literature and connections to the Otherworld, or whether Nodens was a localised deity given to a specific part of the River Severn. Yet further evidence of a statue of an unnamed mother Goddess holding a cornucopia has been discovered in Nodens temple that may personify the River Severn. Perhaps this is the Goddess Sabrina who, alongside Nodens, represents a divine union and the fertile nature of the river. After all many votive offerings were found within this temple related to aid in pregnancy. Or Maybe Sabrina is the result of fusion between the two to become the Goddess we know today. Regardless, all these deities are part of the story of Sabrina who transcends categorisation, evolving over time just as her waters continually flow.

Divine Mother

As centuries past, what remained of Sabrina, or any Pagan notion of divinity became subordinate to the rising dominance of Christianity. The land became vacant of former roots; weeded out by promises of salvation and eternal glory from the churches that spread down the river. While I don't want to focus too much on this, at the risk of making suspicious Pagans pick up their pitchforks and accuse me of, dare I say it... being Christian, I find it fascinating the number of churches constructed and dedicated to the Virgin Mary; no less than fifty-eight.[42]

The conversion process of early Britain was not a simple, one directional process of assimilation and eradication of old Pagan Gods, but instead, like with all things related to human belief, a complex and gradual operation.[43] Attitudes assimilated in various manners to the introduction of new theology involving the condemnation of any entities outside its cosmology. Robbed of their home by church teachings, these entities often found their way into the community through folkloric narratives. Christianity also offered similar methods of receiving intercedence from divine sources to that of Pagan Gods, especially through saints, each one equipped to deal effectively with some aspect of life.[44] While the name Sabrina lay dormant, it is apparent that Mary, the Beneficent Queen of Heaven, took a prominent role alongside the River Severn. This doesn't mean Sabrina exists behind the Virgin Mary as a Pagan survival. But what it does indicate is that the river played a central focus for the needs of the people to gravitate towards the mystic maternal waters, and that the beliefs that mattered to the people were likely preserved regardless of who they were praying to. There is also another motherly figure who is associated with the River Severn and has managed to capture the intrigue of those who seek the refuge of a Pagan mother figure. This is no other than Modron, the divine mother.

Modron originally appears as a continuation of the original Gaulish eponym of Matrona who is attached to the River Marne in France, but her most notable appearance is based within the River Severn alongside her son Mabon in the tale of *Culhwch ac Olwen*. We will touch upon Mabon's influence upon the River Severn in a later chapter but to summarise her role, Modron gives birth to the infant Mabon who is then stolen away by an unknown adversary at just three days old. Modron is also mentioned in later texts including *Peniarth Manuscript 147* and *Triad 70* as the daughter of Afallach, a king from the Otherworld.[45] She mingles with the realm of men and births the children of Urien Rheged, a 6th century king of the early kingdom of Rheged within the Hen Ogledd or Old North which today appears as the modern counties of Cumbria and Lancashire. However, it is specifically the tale of *Culhwch ac Olwen* that links her to Sabrina's waters, transporting her from an amorphous past to the Welsh tradition as a supreme sovereign, telluric figure presiding over the sustenance and preservation of the Severn landscape. We see Sabrina's waters once again home to an assortment of Goddesses, each adding a little more to her mythos and deepening our understanding of and appreciation for her.

We have taken an expansive tour so far, from etymology, to the early peoples, and glimpses in Christianity. Still Sabrina's Pagan past remains largely a mystery. If archaeologists uncovered a hidden temple with the Words "Sabrina" carved into the entrance, I would be there at the front of the queue having broken the speed of light to get there. However, even in the absence of physical shrines we have been able to shed much light on the Goddess, even if the picture is a little fragmented.

Though she may not always be so apparent, we know her river has always filled a vital role. But the ancient past is not the end of Sabrina's journey, for the Goddess was reawakened from her slumber, brought back to the people with a new identity and a need to be heard.

Chapter 3

The Poet's Eternal Muse

There is a tenacious beauty displayed by the Goddess. With every conquest and brush of the sword upon the land, Sabrina has stood witness. With every uttered prayer requesting aid, she has emerged from her watery abode to harken to the call. Regardless of speculation surrounding the River Severn's former divinity, her presence was clearly felt among the stoic defenders and brutal invaders that forged the very nature of the Welsh Marches. But it was not war that fully defined her characteristics and granted her immortality. Rather, this rested in the quill of the poets and writers of the ages who thirsted for the former, mythological glories of the land.

Many have taken to paper to recover the hidden paths sculpted by Sabrina, each adorning her with symbols and metaphors to grant the Goddess an eternal resting place. These writings have often been centred around the concepts of national identity, purity, political infringement, bygone quarrels, and chastity. At first this may seem incongruent to the nature of Sabrina's river which embodies more naturalistic and nourishing properties. Yet those who took pity upon the innocent, drowned youth, fashioned her to a more blissful state of existence, invoking her to serve the needs of society beyond her original confines, especially in an age wreathed in chaos and uncertainty.[1] But these literary changes not only adapted the appearance of Sabrina but gave her permanence. Snatched from the snares of the past, the people could once again look upon the river and be captivated by her echoes of sacredness and interconnectedness within all living things. As a result, Sabrina became tangible, as a protective being as well as a virginal nymph, sympathetic to the call of the downtrodden and the blameless and thoroughly preserved in the entanglement of poetry.[2]

Words themselves are immensely powerful, able to empower a nation, to change the course of history or spell ruin for a kingdom and modern stories have equal share of this power as do those of more ancient lineage. They reverberate with a magic that is implicit in each living thing, that omnipotent and primordial force that ensnares the senses for us to embody the animate world around us and to feel its influence in profound manners.[3] Sabrina's writers became the catalyst for facilitating this relationship with the surrounding landscape of her river. As Pagans we can incorporate these into our practice to continue the narrative of Sabrina, for each story operates as a liminal space for us to engage with her along the same energetic streams of inspiration that coursed through those who came before. We can observe the evolution of the Goddess while also constructing our own narratives to give her space to operate within our personal lives. In my Coven we call this unique and transformative force, Awen, which can't be fully translated into English but is taken to mean Holy breath; that which emanates throughout the universe and is internalised by those who tap into its current to breathe it into existence.[4] It is the province of divinity, the fluid spirit of inspiration, poetry, magic, and unity which allowed the remnants of Sabrina to be preserved as a classical figure in literature.

The Dampened Spectre

Geoffrey of Monmouth's tale omitted Sabrina of voice and personhood while subjecting her to turmoil because of her family's foolish conduct. Her father, King Locrinus, became the epitome of lust and instability, and her mother, Estrildis, posed as the indiscreet, seductive power source that tempted the king away from the confines of his previous relationship. Estrildis' body transformed into the vessel to bring forth the threat of ruin to the dynasty in the form of Sabrina, the illegitimate child who was gestated under the earth in her mother's secret lair. There she waited to unknowingly incite a kingdom of violence.[5]

However, Sabrina is later resurrected beyond her watery grave in the collection of poems referred to as *The Mirror for Magistrates*. Compiled by various writers and repeatedly recontextualised to fit the Tudor and Jacobean period between 1559 and 1610, The *Mirror* is an expansive piece which invokes laments, tragedies, and disasters of historical figures as a warning to those in power should they fail to embody the lessons within. This was especially relevant for a time of increased capitalistic enrichment and systematic inequality in property rights[6] which I believe some of our modern politicians could do with a lesson in, less they face the downfall of their predecessors. Sabrina appears in the adaption of Jim Higgins whose narrative voice envisions the Goddess as a cold, dampened and ghastly entity alongside her mother Estrildis as he recounts:

> *So in the waters as I stiu'd to swimme,*
> *And kept my head aboue the waues for breath,*
> *Mee thought I sawe my childe would venter in,*
> *Which cry'd amayne, "O let me take like death".*
> *The waters streyght had drawne me vnderneath*
> *Where diueing, vp at length agayn rose I,*
> *And sawe my childe, and cry'd "Farewell, I die"* [7]

In death she warns the reader to be moral, and diplomatic as it is always the innocent that pays the price in war.[8] The tale of Sabrina's demise continued to catch the eye of several writers who adapted her story to reimagine the Goddess in a unique manner that emphasised her autonomy. This includes the anonymous author of *The Lamentable Tragedie of Locrine* in 1595, which was originally attributed to William Shakespeare but has since been disputed by modern examinations of the text.

Although similar to previous works, Sabrina is instead an active agent. Although she can't prevent the vengeance of Gwendolen, in a moment of bravery she sacrifices herself to the river to illicit a response through martyrdom for the injustice suffered by her mother and father.[9] For such bravery, Sabrina is commemorated by Gwendolen:

> *One Mischief follows on another's neck.*
> *Who would have thought so young a maid as she*
> *With such courage would have sought her death?*
> *And for because this river was the place*
> *Where little Sabren resolutely died,*
> *Sabren for ever shall this same be called*[10]

Sovereign Queen

By the 16th and 17th century, Sabrina underwent further momentous change, influenced by the aftermath of England's increased governance over the administration and culture of Wales under the proclamation of a unified British identity. The Tudors had already suffered heavy pushback on their claim to the throne since the time of Henry VII. To legitimise his and his descendant's future rule, prophetic propaganda and mythological histories were invoked to cultivate the idea that Henry VII was the son of prophecy or Mab Darogan, destined to end the oppression of the native Britons by the invading English.[11] This method continued through to the Elizabethan period which faced an exacerbated fear of fragmentation of the land due to resistance towards its monarch at the time, Queen Elizabeth I.

But in the same manner, the Queen utilised the lands stories to fashion an air of enigma about her reign and to reassure her strength in maintaining its unification.[12] These were popularized by various writers like Edmund Spencer, who made allegorical comparisons between her and other strong, feminine, ethereal characters from history.[13] It would be hard to dismiss the similarities Elizabethan writers would have been met with when influenced by the original stories of Geoffrey of Monmouth. Both Elizabeth and Sabrina could be seen as illegitimate children to fathers who were unsatisfied by one queen. Both were perceived as eternalised virgins with Sabrina's virginity entangled in her tragic and untimely death and Elizabeth's virginity matrimonially tethered to England as its wife, queen, and mother, drawing upon the medieval themes of sovereignty. This is often depicted as a tutelary powerful feminine being.[14] Therefore, the turbulence and friction born from the divisiveness of the Reformation and ecclesiastical outcry between Catholics and Protestants were subdued by the metaphors of aristocratic writers who maintained allegiance to the idea of one British nation.[15]

However, it wasn't until Michael Drayton's *Poly-Olbion* in 1612 that the River Severn was linked to the instability of British identity with Sabrina fully conceptualised as a mother figure to the landscape. This chorographical poem tells the tales of the nymphs and dryads who preside over each territory as its personified representative. Sabrina gains corporeal form as a regal ruler over the Welsh and English rivers that flow into her waters. Yet the poem; the first of its kind to transform Sabrina into a Goddess[16], places her graceful presence amidst the violence and chaos erupting over the ownership of Lundy Island. To resolve this dispute, the Goddess mediates as a neutral judge, giving credence to both claims from the English and Welsh.

My neere and loued Nymphs, good hap ye both betide;
Well Britans have yee sung; you English, Well repli'd;
Which to succeeding times shall memorize your stories;
To either countries praise as both your endlesse glories[17]

As fair, rational and equally as powerful as the Sea God Neptune, Sabrina continues to prophesise of the unification of the land and identity under the reign of the Stuarts who satisfy the bloodline request for the rightful rule. She proclaims Lundy Island belongs equally to both Wales and England.[18]

Then take my finall doome
Pronounced lastlie, this;
That Lundy like Ally'd
To Wales and England is [19]

Poly-Olbion echoes the positive sentiment of one ruling identity influenced by the political state which witnessed the union of the crowns under the reign of King James I and VI's. But at the same time, the merging of identity at the Welsh border increasingly gave rise to feuds and bloodshed with the River Severn, both in history, mythology and in poetry becoming the central place of disunity.[20] The Goddess' affiliation for both sides of her river quickly subsides later on in *Poly-Olbion* with Sabrina grieving for the ancient wrongs done to Wales and its inhabitants, especially for those within the counties of the Marches.

Within the front of Drayton's work, is an acknowledgement that the counties of Shropshire, Worcestershire and Gloucestershire belong to their ancient mother; an opinion that still stands among some of the people of these counties. With the river becoming a perpetual symbol of fragility and dissent, the Goddess, despite gaining new attributes, suffers in silence between writers over a landscape scarred by warfare and conquest. Sabrina becomes mournful of what has occurred and defeated by her attempt to bring the land together which cannot possibly be done due to such drastic differences between people. *Poly-Olbion* itself begs the question what is quintessentially British identity? This question is more relevant than ever today, as many people are turning away from imposed labels to relate more to their collective home and culture. Sabrina has always called her children back to recognise the land under her regulation and to support their claim to a supressed and overlooked oneness in the Welsh Marches that's distinct from the rest of Britain. This piece of work gave birth to the most influential and radical presentation of the Goddess Sabrina as she was revitalised as a protectress living among the shepherds and waves of her river waiting to be invoked.

The Virgin Nymph

Within *Poly-Olbion*, Sabrina occupies a heavy political position mediating the challenges towards the idea of British homogeneity. But her story also shows the Goddess interfering to protect the virgins that live within the Forest of Dean away from the advances of the lustful satyrs. This later influenced the famous writings of John Milton, whose allegorical passages of Christian and Greco-Roman imagery embodied Sabrina as the paragon of purity and virginity.

Comus, formally known as a *Masque* presented at Ludlow castle, 1634, was commissioned as a dramatic performance to celebrate the inauguration of the Earl of Bridgewater as the Lord president of Wales. Yet the emphasis on the Goddess was not placed around the fragmented nature of the geographical allegiance, but instead was placed upon Sabrina's transformation into a gentle, chaste and courageous nymph who is invoked in song to aid those taken by impurity.

The play begins with the Attendant Spirit, disguised as a shepherd, warning the audience of the debaucherous and nefarious nature of Comus. As the offspring of Bacchus and Circe, Comus parades the land as a devilish and powerful figure with an aptitude for enchantment. He delights in disfiguring the local people by turning them into hideous beasts that revel in their dirty nature as his retinue. Later, he encounters The

Lady, who is characterised as the epitome of purity. Captured by his magic and rendered immobile upon an enchanted chair, the two later erupt in dispute between the hedonistic seduction and pleasures of the flesh and the importance of virtue and resistance of temptation in order to remain righteous and pious. However, The Lady is later rescued when her two brothers find the Attendant Spirit who conjures the legendary Goddess:

> *Sabrina fair,*
> *Listen where thou art sitting*
> *Under the glassy, cool, translucent wave,*
> *In twisted braids of lilies knitting*
> *The loose train of thy amber-dropping hair,*
> *Listen for dear honours sake,*
> *Goddess of the silver lake,*
> *Listen and Save!!*[21]

Sabrina, with her powerful and sublime presence rippling through the waves of her river, emerges with her accompanying nymphs to assist the lady, with the Goddess the only entity capable of breaking the spell. With dampened hands, Sabrina sprinkles water across various parts of The Lady's body which allows her to escape, after which Sabrina retreats to the depths of the River Severn; powerful imagery that reiterates the protective virtues of the Goddess towards those who call upon her water, especially if they are in distress.

Despite the unnatural attachment of puritan ideals through the Christianisation of Sabrina's Pagan character, especially with Milton's repetition of her virginal state, the Goddess, who was once confined to an obscure past, had now been dynamically reclaimed. Through the works of those inspired by the vibrant beauty and tragedy of the Goddess' tale, Sabrina found her voice and personhood with each piece of writing a wellspring of fertile information that can facilitate connection and gnosis. While representing the fruitfulness of nature, Sabrina gained a discernible identity that reminds us of the dangers of homogeneity and the loss of the rich context and heritage the land has to offer. Through the ages, Sabrina's invocation challenges us to look at how we identify ourselves, allowing us to break away from the confinement of labels placed upon us and to be free like her river, who will rush to our sides in our darkest hour to remind us that the Goddess is nearby.

The poetry of *Sabrina Fair* is a testament to her survival, as it is not secluded to the work of Milton but lives on in the modern day, fuelled by the experiential connection between Sabrina and those who utter it. Not only is the poem etched on many of her statues for people to pass by and read, but it is also one I use in my personal practice. Each time the words pass on anybody's lips, they are empowered and potent with the power of the Goddess of the translucent wave who is always listening. This may not be the Goddess of antiquity, nevertheless it is the Goddess we have and without the work of the early modern period, Sabrina would have been lost to time. Think of her as you would a river. The water changes constantly but it flows in the same bed. While the stock of lore is ever changing and expanding, Sabrina's essential character remains the same. With this we can now fashion her in our minds eye as the amber haired, riverine nymph.

Chapter 4

Bridge to the Otherworld

Within the hushed hues of twilight, where the violet sky dances upon the River Severn's reflection, a tranquil ambience will frequently assume the land of the Marches. But observe beyond these peaceful moments and a piercing voice may erupt, reverberating with sorrow and despair from a spectral woman caught amidst the continuous waves of the river. Whether she is struggling against the water, or shrouded in fog as she wanders the banks, it is always a beautiful yet eerie figure who always catches the curiosity of the peripheral vision, allowing for the River Severn to be envisioned as a place of otherworldly splendour.

Across multiple traditions, rivers have been attested as the threshold to a parallel world that exists simultaneously alongside our own.[1]

Within Sabrina's Welsh heritage, this Otherworld is commonly referred to as Annwfn; a place that evades a singular definition but nevertheless captivates the mind with its mystifying presence and inhabitants. In Welsh folklore and mythology Annwfn is an enigma; a place accessible through different locations and enveloped in magic, abundance, and liminality.[2] The word itself is difficult to translate into English, however, Ifor Williams interprets Annwfn to mean the "In-world" or the "not-world" with "dwfn" taken to mean world and "an" to mean in.[3] However, other theories have suggested that "an" is a negative and intensifying prefix with "dwfn" taken to mean deep; thus Annwfn is interpreted as "the very deep" with Welsh tales confirming this due to being accessed via hills, underground, within the wilderness, and by water.[4] As with Sabrina, it is likely any singular definition is insufficient.

Annwfn features prominently throughout the oldest native texts within Welsh Tradition, referred to as the four branches of the Mabinogi. This consists of various fantastical kingdoms, or in some depictions a series of islands where death and aging is suspended and where time operates in drastically different manners compared to the everyday world.[5] Though distinct in this lavish manner not afforded to the common person and operating according to its own motivations, the Otherworld is still affected by various seasonal changes where its presence becomes increasingly noticeable. Within Welsh belief, the Otherworld and its inhabitants can be closely felt upon the three Ysbrydnos or spirit nights including Nos Calan Mai, the 30th April, Nos Gwyl Ifan, The eve of St John on June 23rd and Nos Galan Gaeaf, the 31st of October.[6] Annwfn is also conceived as a realm of what can be deemed the "Supernatural" where fairies known as Y Tylwyth Teg dwell alongside other divine rulers. It is also the source of Awen which the Bards could access and be endowed with poetic inspiration.[7]

Although not as frequently mentioned compared to other places of water within folklore, the River Severn still features as a portal to the Otherworld, as seen through the eyes of popular characters cherished by Pagans and witches despite Sabrina herself not being specifically acknowledged. The otherworldly realm of the Goddess is presided over by her ever-watchful presence and populated by beautiful yet terrifying entities, waiting for interaction with an unsuspecting mortal.

Fairy Dogs and Blessed Leaders

The Cŵn Annwfn or hounds of the Otherworld are but one of the many peculiar entities witnessed upon the more rural and lonesome paths near Sabrina's beginning. These spectral dogs, also referred to as Cŵn Bendith y Mamau (Dogs of the blessings of the mothers) as well as Cŵn Wybir (Sky Dogs) are often interpreted in Welsh Folklore as an inauspicious omen that traverses the raging winds on stormy nights in pursuit of the sinful and unbaptised.[8] Although seldomly seen, these hounds are described in a variety of manners. Their most common appearance is with white fur and blood red ears or alternatively fur as black as midnight and large eyes that radiate with an infernal glow. My auntie would often warn me to never go and walk the paths near her house alone unless I wanted to encounter an abnormally large, black dog with glowing eyes like she once did. However, it is their howl that should be feared. According to one account recorded by Edmund Jones in the county of Monmouthshire, the closer the dogs are, the less their howl can be heard, a sound which often foretells of an upcoming death within proximity to the person who hears it.[9]

Interestingly, these hounds were described as inhabiting Pumlumon, the birthplace of Sabrina,[10] which has grown in significance for its attachment to the legendary phenomena known as the Wild Hunt. This infamous, nocturnal cavalcade of phantoms and beast companions manifests during liminal times of the year in pursuit of those close to death or as a sign of impending disaster.

The Wild Hunt features across numerous beliefs, often synthesising with the cultural context it finds itself within. In Welsh Folkloric accounts, this incorporates the otherworldly hounds who accompany a mysterious and enigmatic leader. Depending on which tale is being recounted, the leader is often Gwyn ap Nudd, the wild, stoic ruler of Annwfn and lord of the threshold between life and death.[11]

We know that Gwyn has associations with the River Severn with his father, Nudd, previously mentioned as the transformed name from Nodens who presided over the river. Yet Gwyn is never directly mentioned in relation to Sabrina's origin. Another figure, however, could potentially fill this space and may very well be related to Gwyn, possibly even as an additional epithet of his. Across Yr Wyddfa, Cadair Idris and Pumlumon, the Brenin Llwyd is said to roam on the hunt for unwary travellers who climb too high and unintentionally wander into his domain. The Brenin Llwyd translates to either the grey or blessed/holy king and is an unnerving figure, clad in the mists of the Otherworld.[12] My coven often discusses various folk charms and have noticed that some hint at the Otherworld and its rulers within. An example of this would be the 'credo fechan' or little creed, an invocation of God that was commonly used to drive away harm and misfortune.[13] Yet towards the end of this charm, it alludes to a specific Holy man adorned with a white robe.

Credo fechan, credo lân,	*A Little creed, a holy creed*
credo I Dduw ac Ifan,	*A creed to God and John*
Rhag y dwfr, rhac y tân,	*Against the water, against the fire*
rhag Y sarphes goch ben llydan;	*Against the broad headed red serpent*
Cerddais fynudd ac o'r fynudd	*I have walked a mountain, and from the mountain*
A gwelwn Fair wen a rei gobennydd,	*I could see holy Mary on her bolster*
A'i hangel, angel ufudd,	*and her angel, an obedient angel*
A Dduw ei hyn yn dedwydd,	*and God himself joyous*
Ar gwr llwyd a'i wisc wen yn llunio	*and the holy man with his white robe*
Llen rhwng pob enaid ac uffern	*Drawing a veil between every soul and hell*
Amen[14]	*Amen*

Although commonly thought to be a variation of the holy creed, the involvement of this strange character, combined with the circumstance of the mountain tops and his perceived power of drawing a veil between the souls and Hell which was also a term used synonymously with Annwfn, may pertain to the king of the mists. Therefore, this charm may secretly be drawing on the magical powers of Gwyn ap Nudd, which obliquely connects to Sabrina. Of course, this is speculation and the people at the time using this charm would never have made this link but it's something fun to think about.

Songs of the Merfolk

It doesn't come as much of a surprise to hear tales of merfolk within the riverside communities and angling circles. But compared to other waterscapes across Britian, the River Severn seems to have a scarcity of legends recalling these beautiful yet menacing creatures. In the traditions of the people who live close to the River Severn estuary, lustful, green haired nymphs, otherwise referred to as Sea Morgans inhabit the crashing waves, waiting for the perfect opportunity to sing their bewitching songs to those who get close to their abode.[15] Often, interactions between those of the terrestrial world and those of the aquatic don't have a happy ending. In 1916 folklorist Ruth Tongue recorded an oral tale of a fisherman and his wife who stumbled across an abandoned baby under a waterfall at St Audries Bay on the Severn estuary. Her people had fled for the safety of the ocean after hearing the approaching humans.[16] Setting eyes upon the child, their grief-stricken hearts from the loss of their previous child once again filled with love with the fisherman and his wife taking the child under their wing.

This was no ordinary child however, as with each passing day her behaviour became more peculiar, marking her as other amongst the whispers of the community. Her affinity for water grew ever stronger. She would spend her time paddling within the spring ponds and no matter how hard her mother tried, her hair remained damp and scented with the salty remnants of the sea. One day, after hearing the calls of her people within the waves yonder, the child prophesised of an oncoming storm which allowed the perfect opportunity for the people of Doniford and Staple to pursue her for fear of her power. With haste she easily escaped her attackers and found refuge upon a rock where an almighty wave reached out and pulled her back to the waters she longed for. The child was never seen again.

A similar tales also occurs in the vicinity of Churchdown in Gloucester where the Goddess herself assumes the form of a mermaid; her divine presence blending in with the superstitions of those who feared the treacherous moods of the Severn estuary. Sea morgans were reputed for their combat with fishermen, using conger eels to consume their flesh with one in particular, which some today may call Sabrina, known for her charming songs and homicidal tendencies. But she was eventually defeated one day by a local man who fought off the plentiful eels at Wellhouse Rock off Sharpness, equipped with a secret weapon: his deafness. Unable to enthral him with her songs and consumed with sorrow for her defeat, Sabrina retreated across the waters and returned to the safety of the River Severn bore where she became the presiding spirit.

No one knows how accurate these oral tales are or whether Ruth Jones and other folklorists like Kathrine Briggs took influence from other sources and further fabricated them for dramatic effect. For instance, Morgan is a term in Breton to refer to Mermaids within their tales, as opposed to native Welsh term Môr-forwyn. But where folklore stays silent, the ever watchful, river side churches speak through stone of the memories of these haunting creatures. Glance at the doorway of Bartholomew's Church in Churchdown and you may just come across the graffito of a mermaid holding a square mirror and comb as a reminder of the inhabitants in Sabrina's domain.

A Claw from the Depths

The Otherworld is shrouded in paradox and much like Sabrina, stands as a pervasive, perceptible force of transition through its every changing, encroaching borders. While not explicitly mentioned, Sabrina and her mighty bore may very well feature as a scattered piece of folk memory behind certain characters in the first branch of the *Mabinogi*. During Rhiannon's reprimand for the disappearance of her child, down in the south of Wales, Teyrnon Twrf liant, lord of Gwent Is Coed, suffers the presence of a monstrous claw that steals his foal every May's eve.[17] One night, Teyrnon finally manages to catch a glimpse of the claw in action, forcing its way through the stable windows and latching on to an unsuspecting foal. With one mighty swing of his axe, Teyrnon hacks the monstrous claw off at the elbow with the unseen creature scurrying away in agony.

It is clear, especially with the mystical lore surrounding May Day within past and modern-day folklore, that his foal was being stolen by a force originating from the Otherworld. But on closer inspection, Teyrnon's name may perhaps link this mysterious claw to the powers originating from within the River Severn. Teyrnon Twf liant translates to Divine lord of the raging sea or flood which due to his proximity of his kingdom may reference the River Severn's bore which is well attested as wreaking destruction and pulling the lives of the innocent into its grasps. The lord of the flood slicing the approaching arm may be an interpretation of the ebb and flow of the tides and its power to pull what it wants from this world into its own.[18] This carries echoes of the interpretation of the bore as two battling kings. I can't help but also relate this claw to the oral folk tales of Gloucestershire in which the Druids of the Celtic lands fled across the River Severn to escape Roman persecution. In their desperate attempts to defend their sacred home, the druids assembled and invoked the power of the River Severn bore to surge with incredible power and flood the landscape, thwarting the attempts of the Romans from crossing. Maybe there is more to this than meets the eye when we consider Nodens' connection to the bore and his silver arm combined with the evidence of a bronze arm from within his temple at Lydney; either way there is no denying the impact of the River Severn upon ancient and modern narratives. Whatever the case, an exploration of

Sabrina at least poses some intriguing questions regarding the first branch of the *Mabinogi*.

Gwiddonod Caerloyw

Within the episodic tale of Peredur, Son of Efrawg, which forms one of the three romantic tales often told alongside the four branches of the *Mabinogi*, the protagonist, Peredur, engages in combat with nine malignant witches.[19] These women, possessed of otherworldly magic were said to reside within Caerloyw; the fortress of light which in English refers to the city of Gloucester right next to the River Severn. During his adventures, Peredur descends upon the hall of a well-attended lady who offers her hospitality with caution due to her home constantly being threatened by nine witches. In accordance with his chivalrous nature, Peredur swears to defend her in anticipation of their next suspected attack. At dawn, Peredur's slumber is disturbed by the terrible wails of the watchmen who suffer the attack of one of the witches.

With a mighty swing of his sword, Peredur manages to flatten her helmet, rendering the witch immobile and pleading for his mercy. She reveals that she knew all too well who he was, prophesising his coming and the great adversity he would inflict upon her sisters. As the two negotiated, the witch offered to train him in exchange for her promise to cause no further harm. For three weeks, Peredur resided within the court of the fearsome Witches, absorbing the magical teaching of his formidable mentor alongside a newly selected weapon of his choice and fine horse to aid his journey once his time had passed. However, this peace settlement was not to last due to Peredur discovering the witches had previously killed his cousin and harmed his uncle. With the want of revenge coursing through his veins, Peredur summoned King Arthur and his men to accompany him towards Caerloyw to annihilate the witches once and for all. King Arthur and his men battled bravely against them with

Peredur pleading to their seemingly unconquerable leader to stave off her attacks. However, his request fell upon deaf ears as she continued in her lust for bloodshed. By the time three of Arthur's men had been slaughtered, Peredur swiftly intervened, striking the Witch down with her last cries warning her sisters to flee from the prophesised warrior. Yet her last concerns for her sisters were in vain, as Arthur and his men continued their attack until the last heinous witch was slain.

Groupings of nine women, who exhibit otherworldly powers and live upon the outskirts of a society which deems them as "Other" are particularly prevalent within Welsh Mythology, especially within Arthurian accounts. Many have put forward that this tale reflects a different cultural perspective during the time of Christianity's patriarchal domination, with the witches perceived as a perversion of womanhood and a central point for the hero to be a beacon of virtue and integrity during his mastery over their magic.[20] Nevertheless, the tale shows a strong connection with the River Severn, its once fearsome occupants and the Fortress of Light which perhaps may have been another access point into the Otherworld.

Chapter 5

The Sabrina Folk

Since the beginning of human history, Sabrina has occupied a central position in the formation of her own distinct culture and heritage. Her presence and power have always been regarded with respect with many locals in everyday language referring to her as either Severn or Sabrina.[1] Her river boasts of an active and complex history, employed to fulfil the needs of the people on a local and global scale. Exploring Sabrina's people and their customs is another way to sieve out more fascinating aspects which have been involved in so many developments, one of which includes Sabrina's contribution to the birth of the industrial revolution.

Goddess of Iron and Trade

The economic transition from agricultural productivity to the furnaces of mechanical development gave way to a radical period of change due to an abundance of coal, iron, limestone and clay, manufactured within the Ironbridge Gorge in Shropshire.[2] This alongside the construction of the Ironbridge in 1779 by Thomas Pritchard and Abraham Darby III to support the transportational uses of the River Severn, symbolised the pioneering, smoke filled optimism of the 18th century, all whilst straddling the Goddess' river. Sabrina's waters have always been used for their navigable qualities with the estuary and the shoreside locations the first to give rise to the development of several ports where goods could be traded. This included Gloucester, Tewkesbury, Bewdley, Shrewsbury and Pool Quay. This was all helped by the developing culture of the watermen who had intimate knowledge of the River Severn.[3]

Watermen comprised the crew of various vessels that travelled along the river, distinguished by their broad backs and dress consisting of flannel flocks.[4] From the colour of the water alone they had the ability to tell whether an influx of water originated from the upper Severn or the Vyrnwy and Tanat tributaries.[5] Their life sounds idyllic with the open water and sense of freedom coursing the waves of ambition and dreams, yet a Watermans life often fluctuated between revelry and controversy. If travel upon the river was not possible a Waterman could be found supplementing their income by Morris dancing and could often be found participating in May Day wakes including the infamous traditional fights between countrymen and miners on top of the Wrekin.[6] However, they could also be found frequenting the various pubs, inns and brothels established across the River Severn engaging in excessive drinking and criminal behaviour. If you were to visit Ribbesford Church in Worcestershire or Benthall Church in Shropshire, you may just catch a glimpse of their gravestones marked by the symbol of the anchor.[7]

River transportation, however, slowly declined with the increase in recreational space along with the construction of canals, and the watermen went with it.

Sabrina's banks are the place to be for rowers and anglers, easily recognisable by their cowl shaped coracles, casting their nets and transporting people from one side to the other.[8] The coracle itself was a common sight upon the river, constructed from ash laths that had been soaked in hot water before interwoven and reinforced with animal skin with the Roger's family of Ironbridge the last famous family to traditionally make these handy, lightweight boats in the 19th century.[9] In bygone ages many have swum in Sabrina's river, washed their dirty laundry in her, and drunk from her... which I wouldn't recommend in today's age unless you want a nice cup of E. coli with a dash of chicken faeces. But the past was not always so blissful with river folk unable to escape the tarnishing that accompanied a river associated with boundaries.

Corruption of the Hybrids

The river as a frontier has experienced decades of sporadic raiding, slaughter, burning and rebellion because of England's increased domination over Wales. Due to differences in authority and administration, lawlessness increased amongst the people allowing for the outlaw, the bandit, and the cultural miscreant to flourish under the watchful eye of the Goddess. Sabrina can almost be seen as the mother of the fugitive, with the people of her landscape regularly accused of harbouring law breakers by taking advantage of arddel; the custom of an incomer being granted tenancy by the governing Marcher lords.[10] This then allowed for various hideouts to flourish including Llanymynechs, Coed y Graig Lwyd, the grey rocky woods of Llewelyn ab y Moel who longed for Owain Glyndŵr's prophetic return.[11]

Geographically, the river has always been utilised as a place of defence by multiple groups who have crossed her in the name of war; an unfortunate heritage that stems all the way back to the times of Caratacus, leader of the Iron Age Catuvellauni tribe who fought against the imperial legions of Rome by fleeing across Sabrina and enlisting the help of the southern Silures. From thereon, the Goddess has watched behind from murmuring waves the events of the Anglo-Welsh wars including the battle between Gruffudd ap Llywelyn and Leofric, Earl of Merica at Rhyd y Groes, the seizing of Shrewsbury castle by Llewelyn ap Iowerth and the decapitation of Daffydd ap Gruffudd by order of Edwards I to name a few examples. But it was Owain Glyndŵr, the last medieval individual who bore the title of Prince of Wales who nearly changed the fate of Sabrina's river through his rebellion against the English in the name of Welsh Independence. In 1405, Glyndŵr, alongside his allies

Edmund Mortimer and Henry Percy, agreed to separate Britain into equal parts with the River Severn returned to Wales along with the Welsh Marches, an agreement known as the Tripartite Indenture. This never came to fruition with Owain subsequently defeated in the years to come.

Sabrina also seemed to foster a land of magical belief. The Welsh Marches has always had a proclivity for dramatic acts of cursing, such as the infamous public ritual of Joanna Powell in Herefordshire, who loudly cursed the churchwardens in Welsh by falling to her knees and raising her hands to God.[12] However, compared to other places across Britian, there are considerably less historical records when it comes to specific trials and persecutions against those who dabbled in witchcraft. But the River Severn did not escape the universal fear of supernatural forces wielded by those suspected of a diabolical credence. As we travel down the slopes of Sabrina's winding waters, we find the Welsh Marches is frequented with stories rooted in the belief of maleficium and punishment of those caught up in the accusations. The river was often the designated place to be scolded or publicly humiliated through the device known as the ducking stool. This was reserved for women who spoke out of turn, tradesmen selling tainted food, and those accused of practicing magic, with the victim paraded round the town and later submerged several times which incentivized onlookers to behave.[13]

Eventually the violence subsided due to changes in politics and blending of people, but the river bound identity persisted. This wasn't characterised by the beautiful transformation afforded to the Goddess but was one of repugnance and degradation due to people being perceived as belonging neither to Wales or England, which may have inspired the depiction of the half human half beast horde of *Comus* in the work of John Milton.[14] In summary, those of us who grew up and were influenced by the Goddess' river were seen as law breaking, cursing, cross bred monsters.... but in all honesty, I've been called worse.

Life Giver and Taker

If there is one place the Goddess takes precedence, it is the everchanging cycle of life and death with Sabrina holding the delicate balance in her hands, especially when guiding those deemed as the river born. Across the river, multiple hermitages established themselves with monks taking refuge within the cave systems and helping travellers' cross perilous waters, such as the monks of the Redstone Rock of Stourport in Worcestershire.[15] Downstream, in the town of Bewdley, voyagers would come to Blackstone Rock where the monks would bless their travels. But they would also keep an eye out for any unwanted child that was cast into Sabrina's river. Carried by the tutelary Goddess, the disregarded children were brought to safety and given protection as well as the last name of Severn to forever tether them to the Goddess.[16]

But where life flows, the ghastly, ice cold fingers of death are never too far away, waiting to pull the oblivious and the unfortunate to an eternal aqueous slumber. In Gloucestershire a common belief held is "Sabrina always gets her man", an unnerving foreshadowing of the Goddess' sacrificial hunger with her river infamous for claiming the lives of so many throughout the years.[17] Death upon the River Severn is usually the result of an accident by those who have been intoxicated near her banks or by those who misjudge the strength of her currents, or in the most extreme cases by murder or suicide. In my home it is believed that if a murder was committed in or nearby the river then Sabrina would soon claim the life of the culprit responsible for contaminating her waters.[18]

Yet the cessation of life by the hands of the river does not spell the end of a person's presence. When a candle is extinguished, residual heat and energy linger and in the same manner those who have suffered tragic and macabre endings often become bound to the river. There it becomes the centre point from which to pierce our world and remind us that the deceased are never too far away. Sabrina's river is inundated with spirits, each one accompanied with their own historical context, who illicit profound change when we encounter them. Included are various monks who inhabited the river side cathedrals, Roman soldiers who routinely patrol the wild green meadows, and ghostly children who wandered too far from their parents' watchful eye. The spirits of the River Severn all deserve to be recognised along with their stories for they are another path that connects to the history of the Goddess.

To write about them all would unfortunately extend beyond the confines of this book but there are some which have become ingrained with communal memory from the fascinating to the terrifying.

One story that I frequently encounter is the tale of Mrs Foxall, who is reputed to roam the Dingle; the same place in which I first met a statue of Sabrina. If you go there, you will see a plaque detailing the case of Mrs Foxall, right next to the River Severn. Mrs Foxhall was burnt at the stake for the crime of murdering her husband in 1647. Upon the anniversary of her death, her spirit can be spotted appearing to walk upon the Dingles paths with a distressed look upon her spectral face. It is common to find the space and stillness of death denied to a select few due to such disturbing circumstances. Troubled by their past earthly exploits, spirits often linger around the river, existing in a state of fragility that leaves them stranded between worlds. But they are not without power, for their ferocity is often invoked by their continual restlessness, such as the spirit of Lady Jeffrey of Llanidloes who terrorised many of the town's folk in various forms before she was persuaded to enter a bottle.[19] This was then sealed shut and cast into Sabrina's river under the Llanidloes bridge, there to remain until the ivy growing on each side of the bridge grew to touch each other; a horrific thought that motivated many people to ensure the ivy was kept trimmed.

In many rural areas the trapping of a spirit in a vessel is known as ghost laying, which doesn't fulfil the profile of an exorcism but still renders the ghost incapable of causing harm... most of the time. An attempt at ghost laying once proved unsuccessful for a group of clergy men who tried to dispel the spirit of Captain Thomas Bound; a cruel and vicious man in life who was said to have committed various nefarious acts before he took his own life by drowning in the causeway pool near his home in Upton upon Severn.[20] After trying to exercise his ghost through various incantations and dropping lit candles into the site of his death, Thomas proved to be a more powerful spirit who could often be seen on the banks of the River Severn waiting to scare the local fishermen. If you're lucky and happen to be in the vicinity of Ironbridge you may just catch a glimpse of the Ghost Barge sailing silently down the river, carrying the unholy sight of bodies that had succumbed to the bubonic plague to their final resting place.[21] Sabrina reminds us that she is a place of both life and death; through the destruction wrought upon her banks by her own volition and those caused by the hands of others or on occasion the misfortunes of nature.

New Life, New Land

Throughout this book I have emphasised Sabrina's presence being intrinsically tied to the Marches landscape and its people both in life and in death. How then, can somebody who does not live in proximity or who lives in a different country, connect with a deity who is orientated around the fixed flowing waters of the River Severn? While it is true that specific deities originate within a particular landscape, this does not mean they are restricted. Sabrina is alive and dynamic, able to forge relationships with people wherever they are.

Sabrina is not bound to corporeal form and so does not adhere to the flesh and blood experience of humanity; she can transcend physicality, living in the continuation of culture, belief and tradition even if that means breeching the legendary waters that birthed her. The Goddess is filled with her own desires which many will resonate with to form sacred relationship with her regardless of if they reside in her landscape or not. The founding mythology of the Goddess and subsequent developments are the strong, nourishing roots that give her permanence and wherever the people go, their beliefs will follow.

This is a historical precedent that has taken place for millennia allowing for diverse and beautiful beliefs to flourish within new environments, alongside new experiences to inform personal gnosis. Wherever you are, the Goddess can be felt within the local waterscape, for water connects all living things on this planet. The traditions that form may not necessarily be identical, but they still exude the longing for connection, the need for Sabrina's stories to permeate everyday life to help those find solace within her safe harbour so that they may continue for generations to come. As long as they are respectful and reverent to the ancestral homeland that birthed the Goddess alongside her accompanying traditions and the language of her reality, there's no telling what beautiful experiences await those wanting to connect to Sabrina.

In 1857 Sabrina emigrated to the land of the star-spangled banner in the form of a 350-pound bronze statue which was gifted to Amherst College by Joel Hayden, the future lieutenant Governor of Massachusetts. Here the Goddess took refuge amongst the frivolity of student life. Sabrina was cherished for her divine presence with Professor John Genung at the time describing her as a *"Divinity, fair and gracious, a gentle protectress who herself deigns to be protected"*.[22] However, Sabrina was not to enjoy the peace for long. In 1860 her feminine guile inspired a mischievous student to adorn her in stolen undergarments form a nearby girls school, as well as with a dent in her cheek from one furious swing of an axe after he was reprimanded. However, this act inspirited the college to perform multiple pranks upon the statue as well as a tradition involving odd and even years to battle it out for the possession of the Goddess.

This rivalry caused such a controversy with Sabrina's poor statue left damaged, tarnished, and transported to several different locations by the attempts of the class to steal her away, including the roof of the octagon, the college well, a barn, the Connecticut river, a sausage factory and dangling mid-air from a helicopter flying across the home coming game of 1989. The tradition continued for many years sometimes ending in disastrous outcomes including various fights and injuries. Sabrina was titled the champion of the even years, spending many a time residing over the feasting banquets while the students pledged their allegiance to her. I can't help but see a similarity in the contention between the students over the goddess with the people who spent years fighting over the boundary disputes of the River Severn in the Marches. Many saw this as defiant and rooted in sexism while others deemed it a mystical and significant act which fostered loyalty and fellowship amongst the dull and demanding lives of students. The Goddess nevertheless sits at the heart of the Amherst college, presiding over memory and hearts of the alumni who sing:

Sabrina fair, Sabrina, dear,
We raise to thee our hearty cheer,
Come fellows, all, and give a toast
To her we love, and love the most[23]

Chapter 6

Sacred Animals

Animals offer a fascinating window into the divine. Anne Ross suggests the way deities are perceived emerges from the importance of an animal's form within various Celtic cults.[1] Whether Sabrina did shed a past animal form or not, she certainly has a retinue of sacred animals that capture an aspect of her divinity today. They are teachers, enhancing our capacity to understand ourselves in relation to our other-than-human family and to the Goddess. Sabrina does not have a formal list of animal correspondences, however, throughout history and in my own personal practice, multiple species tend to show up. Each of these animals I will discuss here offer access to different aspect of Sabrina and her nature.

The Swan

If there is one animal considered the most sacred among all Sabrina's dearest it is the elegant swan. It's nearly impossible to walk the route of the River Severn without setting eyes upon the bird which graciously glides upon her waters, contributing to the serene beauty inherent in the river and dispersing nutrients to the ecosystem. In fact, there are various areas across the River Severn which have been dedicated to preserving their environment including the swan sanctuary in Worcestershire. These sanctuaries are further supplemented with food given by the locals as an everlasting bond between the people and the river inhabitants. Swans are timeless creatures of fairy tale and lore, symbolic of life's perils and curses lurking behind their pale wings, featuring in stories of princesses and maidens confined to avian form by the hands of malicious enchanters. This theme of transformation also reflects Sabrina's origins, being transformed from a drowned princess into a mighty river Goddess.

In my personal craft, swans are revered as Sabrina's messengers, embodying both beauty and tragedy. Their fair appearance is also reminiscent of their otherworldly connection, for it is through the blue world, the river, the lake, and the mist, that the Gods dwell and that swans and the lost souls of the River Severn congregate together in the tranquillity of Sabrina's waters. Whenever I communicate with Sabrina, without fail a swan appears. I have had many encounters with the bird growing up near the River Severn, feeding them on days out with my family and watching them preen themselves. The most phenomenal encounter I ever had occurred when I was 17 years old.

Walking along the tree ladened path next to the River Severn in Shrewsbury, Shropshire, I was overcome with a nagging feeling. Something kept urging me to turn towards the river banks, to a particular section that had been secluded under a veil of overhanging willow branches. Whilst sitting patiently underneath, away from the public eye with access to the water, I plunged my feet into to feel its cold revitalising energy and decided to call out to Sabrina. I had already been practicing witchcraft on and off for a few years, dabbling with failed attempts at love spells on the odd celebrity here and there but never truly engaging with the magic that was already inherent within my home. I had grown up with the stories of Sabrina, and always said hello to the river but never truly interacted with the Goddess like this before.

I summoned the courage to call out. At first a silence extended across the water which I took to be a bad sign, especially being an angsty teenager. I closed my eyes again and called out with all my heart for the Goddess to reassure me she was there. To my surprise, after opening my eyes, a pair of swans appeared with one jumping out of the river to sit next to me. I didn't know whether to shriek with joy or to be concerned because of their stereotypical aggressive behaviour and the whole "Swans can break your arm" narrative. They stayed with me while I basked in their ethereal aura. I knew Sabrina was with me and later in the night, caught betwixt the worlds of dreams and reality, I again was sat by the River Severn and saw a woman of lithe, blue skin emerging out of the river. Damp saffron hair dangled gently upon her shoulders, caressing the sides of her face into a mirage of sophistication and benevolence. Like a concerned mother, she approached me and placed her hands upon my shoulders, whispering to me words that have been imprinted upon me up until this very day:

"Remember me as I remember you; I am here if you need me"

From that moment on I make it my personal practice to visit the River Severn as much as possible to feed Sabrina's swans, which earns me a variety of looks from onlookers who wonder why my bag sometimes smells of fishy wheat pellets mixed with a hint of frozen peas. What better way to establish a relationship with the Goddess than by feeding her animals and if I'm lucky they'll grant me the privilege of their company along with three honks to express gratitude for the food. Of course, I do not suggest approaching any swan in honour of Sabrina, after all they are wild animals that must always be respected, and swans have been known to be territorial during mating season. But swans recognise the kindness of people and like all animals, they deserve to be treated well which the Goddess of the river will always appreciate.

Much folklore exists upon her banks about these beautifully tragic beings. In Welsh folklore, it is believed that the swan has such an aversion to their own feet that if they catch sight of them, even for a second, they perish from sickness.[2] Swans are usually considered silent for most of their lifetime but upon its death, the swan will sing the most beautiful and haunting tune to be carried upon the wind referred to as the "Swan Song".[3]

Another tale related to these magnificent birds was also described in the works of Lady C Gaskell.[4] Upon a fine and promising day, a nearby queen and her seven sons became lost after successfully hunting two foxes upon horseback. Although previously warned by her husband to never cross the River Severn after it floods, for the spirits are filled with strength and malice, the queen had no choice but to cross its waters. Before reaching the other side, the queen and her children were suddenly seized by the spirits of the river and dragged to the depths, only then to be issued a curse by a nearby witch. The queen and her horse were tragically transformed into a rock while her sons were transformed into seven swans and their horses into seven frogs. The king mourned the loss of his family and fervently sent out a search to find them. Yet it was not the magic of an enchanter or the heroic deeds of a knight that came to his aid, for it was the kindness of his only daughter that brought the family back. Stumbling into the woods, the princess came across a hare who had injured its paw. After binding it in her handkerchief the hare took her to the base of a tree where her swan brothers were circling in flight. Despair cast over her like a shadow, but the hare gifted her a piece of mistletoe for her to wear near her breast. After doing as the hare commanded, the creature vanished, and the swans suddenly transformed back into her regal and dashing brothers. The princess was elated and with her mistletoe in hand she rubbed the plant over the rock which brought her mother and her horse back from their mineral prison. However, some still say the echo of the prince's time as swans can still be heard upon the river as a warning for anyone nearby to be vigilant for the witch who lives nearby.

The Salmon

When discussing Sabrina's waters, it would be unjust not to mention the miscellany of fish who glide through the river's bubbling torrents. It is impossible to comprehend the nature of the Goddess and the surrounding landscape without first contemplating her fish and their role in our everyday lives as well as the rich network of mysticism that pulsates throughout the aquatic community. While fish have continued to form a staple piece of many people's diets, beyond the dinner plate their symbolism thrives as both wanderers and voyagers of the vast, open blue, entangling us and our early ancestors into the connective waters of the depths where the chthonic and otherworldly thrive.

The River Severn boasts of a multitude of species with around 111 blossoming in the estuarian environment alone.[5] This includes sea trout, herrings, lampreys, mackerel, eels etc as well as the odd exotic visitor who can be found roaming Sabrina's waters including Sunfish and bottlenose dolphins. Much to the surprise of the people at the time, in 1885, a gigantic whale unfortunately washed ashore near Littleton, a sensation that is still remembered today with the site known as Whale Wharf. Yet the most prominent of all species, earning it the title of king of all fishes, is the mighty salmon otherwise known as a Molly in some Severn districts.[6] Each year the salmon embarks on an arduous and unforgiving journey, encountering various obstacles from anglers to weirs to return to the shallow spawning grounds which they came from to initiate the life cycle again for a new generation; a fulfilment of evolutionary purpose known as homing.[7] A subtle but pervasive magic shrouds this remarkable fish for it to complete this. The salmon can traverse several domains including fresh and salt water as well as the realm of sky as they leap over any obstacles present in their upstream migrations. One can imagine the nimble display of dazzling silver that captivated all those lucky enough to witness it in the past.

The salmon embodies a feeling that all of us can relate to, especially in times of loneliness, the call for home. As salmon are imprinted with navigational memory to return to the river, so are we imprinted with the embrace of our home, the landscape that holds us and lingers deep inside, calling us back when we strive too far away from its confines. To me, the Salmon is the emblem of my home, where the Goddess Sabrina resides and beckons all to come to her waters and feel rejuvenated. You only have to be near water for it to calm and soothe your physical self with every ebb and flow a reminder of the source of life. It is these attributes together with the salmon's affinity for the River Severn that facilitated its portrayal as the emblem of ancient wisdom within the Celtic continuum; a creature who has witnessed each successive aeon and holds the key to the entrance of the Otherworld.

Within various tales across different regions, the Salmon is repeatedly named as one of the oldest and wisest of all animals[8] with one of these famously having taken place in the southern end of Sabrina's waters. This specifically corresponds to number 26 of the anaethu or impossible tasks in the Welsh story of *Culhwch ac Olwen*.[9] To win the hand of his fated lover, Culhwch had to deliver one of the three exalted prisoners of the island of Britain Mabon ap Modron[10] who was stolen from his mother at three nights old with his whereabouts remaining unknown. Various companions were appointed by Culhwch's cousin King Arthur, each one displaying a heroic and magical quality essential for completing the tasks. To search for Mabon, King Arthur picked his two most trusted men. First was Cai, who possessed the ability to go without sleep or water for nine days, could produce heat from his hands and grow as tall as the trees whenever he wished and could deliver a fatal and incurable blow from his sword. Next was the one-handed

Bedwyr, a handsome and formidable warrior who wielded a magical spear.

Other companions were also selected, including the shapeshifter Gwrhyr Gwalstawd Ieithoedd, the interpreter of tongues who could converse with every living animal, and Eidoel son of Aer who had previously been released from imprisonment. Together with combined strength and magic, they swiftly searched for the oldest animals of the world who retained the memory of Mabon and his potential whereabouts. Gwrhyr greets each animal the same, asking if they know the location of Mabon, including the Blackbird of Cilgwri, the Stag of Rhedynfre and the Owl of Cwm Cawlwyd, with each animal deferring to the knowledge of the next. However, when the men reach and converse with the Eagle of Gwernabwy, the most widely travelled of all, the search party are directed to their destination: the Salmon of Llyn Llyw who almost drowned the eagle after its failed attempt to snatch it up from the water.

Upon being approached and asked the whereabout of Mabon, the humble salmon replied:

....*With every flood time I travel up the river until I come to the bend in the wall of Caerloyw; never before in my life have I heard as much wickedness as I found there*[11]

By recalling the awful injustice, the salmon obliged the men in their quest, offering both Cai and Bedwyr to ride upon its shoulders to where the laments of Mabon could be heard from within his prison. To release Mabon from Caerloyw or modern-day Gloucestershire, King Arthur's men were summoned to attack with Cai demonstrating his superhuman strength by tearing through the walls and rescuing Mabon upon his back. Where exactly did this Salmon of knowledge emerge from? Many attempts have been made to locate the mysterious Llyn

Llyw yet a consensus has yet to be reached. Despite this many clues are given within various medieval texts, including the Historia Brittonum, which describes the body of water as wonderous and similar to an inlet which swallows the water to form a whirlpool close to the River Severn's tidal bore.[12] Likely candidates have been suggested including Chepstow, Llymon brook as well as various places across the marshlands of Gwent. Still, the Salmon evades us along with the added difficulty of unpicking the river's topographical changes.[13]

One thing is certain, however, namely the inherent power contained within the salmon which resonates with an ancient legacy of bridging the physical world with the world of otherness. In this realm, those who dared to adventure could seek the wisdom and sanctity of water through its zoomorphic representations. As *Culhwch ac Olwen* adapted from the oral age of the Cyfarwydd or storytellers, to the written narrative, the tale itself never lost its emphasis that the salmon alongside each animal reminisces of a time where the boundaries between human and animal were non-existent. It speaks of a time when they were respected as part of the landscape's consciousness.[14] Each of the oldest animals can be located upon a map, but it is the oldest and wisest that is linked to the River Severn.

The Pig / Boar

It may seem peculiar to associate a river Goddess with wild or domesticated pigs, but our porcine friends allude to a world of magic; each trotter marking the sacred landscape as a fertile source to extrapolate bestial and otherworldly wisdom. Although linked to stereotypical images of greed, filth, and slovenliness, Welsh medieval literature paints the pig as a prominent representative of the supernatural sphere, with their image acting as a potential and traceable link back to older sacred narratives between humans and the divine.[15] This is evidenced by the adoption of pigs in heraldry as symbols of power as well as their invocation in iconography with additional symbolism of fertility, ferocity, and prosperity in the world of the Celts.[16]

Their magical qualities extend beyond the confines of the medieval period. Within my regional folklore, pigs are ascribed various magical abilities, especially being able to see the wind.[17] Those who drank the broth made from the boiling of bacon would also acquire this gift too. Bacon could also be used for sympathetic transference in which an ailment or wound is removed from the sufferer to an item to speed up the healing process. However, the lore also states that pregnant individuals should avoid being frightened by pigs or else the unborn child would take on its resemblance... which, in hindsight, explains a lot of the appearances of the bullies who attended my school.

Pigs are also important in tales of adventure, actively leading the charge in most narratives with the hero seeking to capture or follow,[18] serving as the catalyst of the tale. There are two pigs pivotal to the lore of the River Severn. The first is Henwen, the old blessed or white sow, who was prophesised to bestow both auspicious blessings as well as inconceivable horrors upon the land.[19] According to Triad 26, Henwen formed part of one of the three powerful swineherds of the island of Britain, cared for by her faithful companion Coll, son of Collfrewy, pig keeper for Dallwyr Dallben in Cornwall. Before Henwen could give birth, King Arthur caught wind of the forthcoming destruction marked by her presence and sent forth his men to destroy the pig and her cursed womb. Henwen frantically raced to the north of Cornwall accompanied by Coll, escaping to the cliff of Penrhyn Awstin (the Aust cliff) before she plunged herself into Sabrina's waters. For many miles, Henwen swam through the currents before she arrived upon the south coast of Wales. From there the fecund pig delivered multiple offspring as she traversed the landscape. This Included:

- A grain of wheat and a bee in Maes Gwenith in Gwent
- A grain of Barley and a bee at Llonion in Pembrokeshire
- A wolf cub and young eagle at the hill of Cyferthwch in Eryri
- A kitten on the black rock in Llanfair

Henwen marked South Wales as with the wonders of the harvest, affording the counties with the best grain and honey whereas the North suffered ill-fated offspring, above all the monstrous kitten, which was thrown into the Menai straits before being fostered by the sons of Palug to later become one of the three great oppressions of Môn.

The second to be associated with Sabrina's river is the legendary and vicious boar known as the Twrch Trwyth who laid a devastating siege to Ireland, Wales and Cornwall, as well as to King Arthurs retinue during the culmination of *Culhwch ac Olwen*.[20] Despite being a force of frenzied reckoning, the murderous beast did not originate this way. This porcine guise was forced upon the son of Taredd Wledig as punishment from God for his sinful behaviour. The Twrch Trwyth possessed a pair of scissors, a razor and comb between its ears which needed to be obtained as part of Culhwch's tasks. The boar was located in Ireland alongside its seven offspring, and here the attack was initiated. King Arthur and his men managed to drive the Twrch Trwyth and his piglets from Ireland across the sea to the south of Wales where for many days and nights he fought against Arthur and his men. Eventually the boar was subdued at the mouth of the River Severn. Both razor and scissors were snatched before he managed to escape to Cornwall. Once there King Arthur managed to overpower the mighty boar, securing hold of the comb whist the Boar was driven into the sea once again.

Between both pigs the boundaries between the land of Arthur and the Otherworld intermingle; a world that is filled with magic and transformation as signified by the pig's supernatural quality.[21] Both pigs emerge from the River Severn with Henwen's fertility both a blessing and curse in the same manner the floods of Sabrina will usher creation and destruction in the same cycle, whereas the transformative aspects of the Twrch Trwyth continue to emphasise the connection between human and beast. Sabrina may not be overtly acknowledged within the origins of these medieval tales yet her presence as a Goddess who yields remarkable power can be substantiated by the presence of these pigs who are both redolent of divinity.

The Sheep

Sheep are one of my favourite animals. Growing up in the Welsh Marches, I spent a large proportion of my time surrounded by fields teeming with walking clouds, each one with a unique personality. Some were stubborn and wouldn't hesitate to headbutt you into oblivion, while others were timid. The vast majority, however, were friendly and would wag their tails like excited dogs if you scratched the right spot behind the ear. Sheep are often viewed as nothing more than empty headed commodities that flock together in times of fear, even if this spells ruin for the group. But this robust animal has extensively shaped the course of human history, dutifully supplying wool to clothe our backs and to tie our communities to Sabrina.

During the medieval period, the woollen industry economically thrived thanks to the best quality wool produced across Wales and the Marches distributed by the Shrewsbury Drapers Company.[22] But according to the work of John Dyer in 1757, these were more than just your average mundane product, but were enriched with the divine essence of the Goddess. In his poem titled *The Fleece*, he mentions a large variety of sheep shearing festivities that took place across the River Severn, with sheep ritualistically dunked into the river to be granted protection from Taint worm and the poisonous leaves of penny grass and spearwort by the presiding Goddess. The poem also highlights the folk custom of propitiating Sabrina with the offerings of sweet-smelling flowers; a joyous and reflective action that honoured the same miraculous ability of the River Severn to distribute an assortment of flower seeds across her land.[23]

> *Sabrina, guardian of the crystal flood,*
> *Shall bless our cares, when she by moonlight clear*
> *Skims o'er the dales, and eyes our sleeping folds:*
> *Or in hoar caves, around Plynlymmon's brow,*
> *Where precious min'rals dart their purple gleams*[24]

Regardless of whether this poem was drawing upon a real or imaginary folk custom, the river is still paramount to the land. Sabrina is the initiator of the changing season, marked by new floral life and the emergence of lambs who with each bleat rejoice in the sanctuary built by her encircling river. This same river lingered within their wool to be then transformed into the products of society with the Goddess living amongst us, hidden yet within reaching distance. In my own personal practice, I often use the list of flowers supplied by the poem as offerings including pale lilies, roses, pink flowers, violets, burnet, mint and thyme. These are perfect to give to Sabrina as they cause no harm to the river and continually link me with the traditions of the land.

Chapter 7

Working Magic with Sabrina

Together we have traversed the ancient world, winding through the memories of the shires where echoes of Celtic mystery and Roman piety slumber. We have rummaged through the tales of the Romantic poets where Sabrina's presence is clearly felt. We have witnessed war, conquest, joy, peace, and grief as well as the ethereal and the mundane converging together in Sabrina's streaming waters. From all of this, we can conjure various pieces of information that can aid us in understanding the Goddess which in turn will give us the foundation to inform our practice.

Connecting with Sabrina is a profound experience accessible to all who seek out her divine presence. At the heart of any Pagan practice is the fostering of relationships with the divine which is based upon respect, effort and reciprocity. An authentic practice does not require reconstructing Sabrina's past, but it does require acknowledgement of divinity that has been here since the first votive offerings, as well as full immersion into the folkloric accounts. Most importantly, a relationship with Sabrina needs a committed and open heart that is receptive to her virtues and wisdom and eagerly ready to experience the Goddess in the here and now.

I have offered several examples throughout this chapter for you to cultivate a relationship with Sabrina but ultimately there is no right or wrong method to achieve this. Always do what feels right to you as this will yield stronger outcomes. My relationship with Sabrina has been something I have grown up with and is expressed via the strands of witchcraft which will look drastically different to those who do not incorporate witchcraft into their lives, and this is perfectly ok. In my practice, I worship Sabrina rather than work with her which may raise a few eyebrows as worship is often equated with subjugation and submission. But to me, my worship does not express itself in the lowering of myself to a dogmatic being but instead actively reflects heartfelt gratitude to a power that has existed for a very long time and has always been there throughout my life, which I see as worthy of respect and my pledge. If you prefer to work with the Goddess that is fine as long as it comes from a place of respect and mutual exchange, after all Sabrina is no dispenser of wish fulfilment but an animate, autonomous being who, like all things on this planet, requires consideration and thoughtful engagement. My practice as a folk witch with Sabrina is bound up in magic and spell work, of which I have also included a few examples.

Some may question how they can establish a connection with Sabrina due to geographical restrains. As we have previously explored, being close to the River Severn is not necessary since Sabrina has travelled beyond its confines and nestled within the historical consciousness of locations far across the ocean. She is not restricted by physical boundaries; the Goddess can always be felt in any landscape that contains water. Her story of travelling along with her sisters demonstrates how far-reaching the influence of the Goddess is, from marshy peat bogs, to rivers, to each droplet of rain.

If you want to initiate a relationship with Sabrina, the best pace to get started is through devotional practice. This includes studying material based on the Goddess to learn her roots as well as her wider influence on the culture of the Welsh Marches. As Sabrina is born between two nations, one devotional method can include learning about Welsh culture and its beautiful language. Unfortunately, even though I grew up both in Wales and in Shropshire in a mixed Welsh and English family, I never got the opportunity to learn Welsh growing up. To honour Sabrina and the history of my home, the Welsh Language plays an important role in my work and with the help of my Coven

I have included a few pieces in this chapter. After all, Welsh is the language of magic, poetry and dragons, who wouldn't want to speak it? I will say as a warning, to never petition Sabrina aimlessly, or for fun as you may be on the receiving end of her temperament. I have heard countless stories of a flooded landscape or house during ritual which reinforces the notion that water and its presiding deities must be respected

Practice: Seeking Sabrina Meditation

To experience the transformative properties of water, especially Sabrina's river, is to experience the magic and mystery inherent within human physiology. The realm of Sabrina exists not only in the external but also within each one of us; never separated but perpetually surging through our veins with sustaining life force. To connect to her and to feel her presence, the best thing you can do is to be in contact with water. This can be the actual River Severn itself or, if not possible, your nearest river or water source. This can also include swimming in wild waters, if it is safe, and you can do so comfortably in permitted spots, or simply connecting with its life-giving energy. Spending time in its company while actively reflecting on the Goddess will enhance your connection to her and usher in profound revelations. Of course, not all of us have this opportunity, especially if our home is devoid of wild flowing water, however, even a bowl that contains water at home still carries this sacredness. It may have come from your tap but think how far this water has journeyed to be inside your bowl, the mighty oceans it has travelled across, the beautiful land it has nourished, the contact it has established between yourself and your thirst. Where there is water there is Sabrina.

For this exercise, if it is possible for you to do so, seek out your nearest river or water source and position yourself comfortable and safely upon its edges during a time when it is not busy. Depending on weather conditions you may wish to take a blanket with you to wrap around yourself or to sit upon. Alternatively, if you can't access water outside, fill a bowl with water and either sit, lie next to, or stand in front of it, whichever works best for you. Bring your attention to the water in front of you and notice its behaviour, whether it is still and motionless or cascading with rhythmic movement. Its fluid nature allows adaptation to any shape it pleases and in the same manner we can adapt to certain situations. Take time to be in this moment, breathing deeply and focusing your senses upon the water until you feel calm and relaxed. Raise your hands upwards and repeat these words in English or in Welsh:

Hafren, Duwies yr afon	*Sabrina, Goddess of the river*
Dwi'n galw i ti	*I call out to thee*
Amddiffynnydd y dyfroedd sanctaidd	*Protector of the sacred waters*
Bydd yma gyda fi	*Be here with me*
Rwy ti'n llifo trwy'r tir	*You who flows through the land*
Rwy ti'n curo yn fy' ngwythiennau	*You who flows through my veins*
Clyw fy llais, a	*Hear my voice, and*
Dalia fi yn dy freichiau	*Embrace me within your domain*

If you wish to do so, and only if it is safe and not polluted, place your hands into the water and feel its embrace upon your skin. Feel the divide between yourself and the water melt away, a feeling indescribable by words yet ever so present within awareness. Close your eyes and take a moment to ponder Sabrina. See her swimming within her river in your mind, flowing through the land and following the path of least resistance. See her meander like a wise old serpent, weaving in and out, shaping the land to her will, carving deep valleys, and settling upon the surrounding meadows to bring nourishment to the plants that thrive upon her banks. Her damp amber hair caresses the sides of her face, her lithe, blue tinted body, swings side to side with each wave while she appears at peace and at one with the water.

Feel her power and might, crashing through any mechanical confines and bursting with energy that ripples throughout the ground. As you continue to visualise, see Sabrina come closer towards you, sending her water to you, up through your hands all the way to the base of your body. It pulsates, pushing its way in to your veins with a cool and soothing sensation. As it travels through your body, working its way through your legs, your stomach, your arms, and your chest, in all directions, feel this water culminate together and circle around your heart. Keep inhaling and exhaling and as you do, notice you are safe in this moment; the water that encapsulates your heart round and round in spiral motion is the water of Sabrina. It reminds you that you are human, and to be human is to feel emotion in all its vibrancy. Whether its happiness, sorrow, fear, or anticipation, your emotions are valid and like a tight and comforting hug upon your heart, visualise Sabrina's flowing river reflecting your emotions. How do you feel in this moment? What sensations are bubbling within your body? What emotions are you experiencing. Whatever you feel, know that Sabrina's water feels the same. You are one whole, beating and flowing together in this shared moment away from the pressures and demands of society.

Sit with this moment as long as you like, taking note of any messages or images that may come to you and when you're ready, feel this water unravel from your heart and wind its way back down your body back to its source. As it dissipates and returns to the Goddess in the river, focus on your breathing and see the Goddess smile at you with a warming smile that shall ever remain with you. You have made contact, you have been welcomed, you have been nourished and you have been reminded that she is always with you. When you feel comfortable open your eyes. Take your hands out of the water and place them on the back of your neck. Feel the revitalising sensations as it brings your senses back to the present moment. Thank the Goddess for any messages, feelings or visions she may have bestowed on you and give an offering in return. This can include cleaning up any rubbish, singing a song or reciting a piece of poetry you may have written beforehand as well as scattering bird seed for the local birds. Feel free to repeat this at any time as frequent engagements with the Goddess only serves to strengthen the connection.

Exercise: Constructing Caerdroia

Meditation and visualisation can prove difficult for certain people. There is nothing wrong with that: different methods work for different people. But if you need help establishing communication a seven-fold labyrinth can be used to guide you towards Sabrina. This ancient symbol, known as a Troy Labyrinth, Troy Town or Caerdroia, has been utilised in a variety of ritualistic practices including as a tool to induce altered states of consciousness. But what does this have to do with Sabrina? If we refer to Chapter 1 you will remember that Sabrina is the granddaughter of Brutus, the legendary exile and leader of the Trojans who established Britain. Although this myth was recorded by the famously unreliable Geoffrey of Monmouth, the mythic link is still captivating and can be used to our advantage. I first came across this labyrinth when I visited a statue of Sabrina in Llanidloes. There she stood, tentatively watching her river and right next to her was a standing stone with the symbol carved on it, which after giving it a go, produced an unexpected but wonderful encounter with the Goddess.

You will need:

- A surface to carve out the design of your labyrinth. This can be a piece of slate that's slightly bigger than the width of your hand, a large, smooth stone, clay or a piece of paper.
- An item to engrave the labyrinth design. If using slate, you can use an engraving pen. If using clay, you can sculpt this with your fingers. If using paper or the stone method, all you will need is a felt tip or paint.
- Incense to consecrate the labyrinth. Consecration is important as it dedicates the tool to the task, imbuing it with a sacred purpose that is seperate from the mundane. In Chapter 6, the poem titled The Fleece referred to the folk custom of appeasing Sabrina via sweet smelling flowers. In my own practice I have experimented with different types and have found a recipe that Sabrina likes, or at least she hasn't turned her nose up at. This includes:
  ○ 2 parts pine resin
  ○ 1 part mint
  ○ 1 part thyme
  ○ 1 part rose
  ○ 1 part lavender
- Charcoal disk
- Fireproof container
- lighter

Method:

- Using which ever method you have selected, carefully etch, paint, or draw the labyrinth design using the guide below.

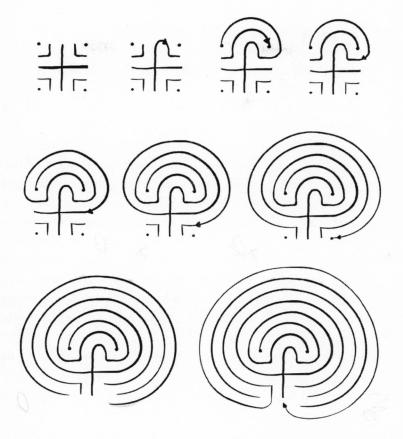

- When you are happy with the design, light your charcoal disk and place it into the fireproof container.
- Grind, the herbs together and take a pinch of the incense. Place it on to the charcoal disk and when it produces enough smoke, pass your labyrinth through it and say:

Sabrina fair, aid me now
This tool, with your grace endow
Mystery swims in depths below
Through the spirals I shall go
For you I now set apart
This tool of my sacred art

- Perform the seeking Sabrina meditation but instead of placing your hands into the water and closing your eyes, dip your finger into the water and start at the entrance of the labyrinth.
- Gently rock back and forth and slowly run your finger through its twists and turns while chanting the same incantation from the meditation. As the labyrinth spirals you further towards the centre, feel your conscious shift. Feel Sabrina guiding your hand and leading you to the centre. With your finger still traversing the labyrinth, let your mind focus on Sabrina and her water as you are chanting.
- Once you have reached the centre and your awareness is focused, close your eyes and take note of any messages, sensations or occurrences that may come up. This way the labyrinth leads you to the liminal space where Sabrina resides.
- When you are finished, take a few deep breaths and allow your awareness to shift back to the present moment, acknowledging your physical body. Ensure you have taken enough time to feel grounded and to record what you experienced whilst thanking Sabrina.
- To dispose of the incense after you're finished, allow it to extinguish and cool or to speed things up, pour water over it. This can then be discarded into a non-flammable container.

Constructing an Altar to Sabrina

Whether it's for elaborate operations or simple acts of piety, altars are considered personal and effective centre points for mystical exploration. Their versatility allows them to be constructed in various styles for both honouring specific deities as well as for performing transformative magic with their aid. Each altar is unique to each individual and deity they are in relationship with, strengthened by physical correspondences and iconography to further embrace their presence. A Sabrina altar will undoubtedly permeate with the ardent, intuitive and cyclical energy of water. An altar doesn't need to be sprawling or covered with every item you can possibly imagine. As long as it is situated somewhere where you can sit comfortably and engage with away from disturbance, the altar can be any size and placed upon a table, a bedside cabinet, a shelf or even a windowsill. An altar dedicated to Sabrina may include:

- **Representative items:** Though it is very rare to come across a statue of Sabrina, substitutes can be used instead including pictures of the river Severn, or pictures of the various sculptures scattered across the Marches. Statues of nymphs can also do the trick especially since they relate to her mythos. Alternatively, if you're artistically inclined, creating a devotional piece can be seen as a beautiful and thoughtful method within your sacred space. Upon my own altar to Sabrina, I have crocheted a stereotypical Goddess figure but have blessed its wool in the waters of her river to consecrate it.
- **Natural correspondences:** Rocks and stones gathered near a river make wonderful allies in connecting with Sabrina; each one filled with their own spirit and the memory of the water's gentle touch during their creation. Always be respectful, they are not just decoration pieces but entities that deserve regard and care to facilitate connection with the Goddess. Be sure to ask permission before taking them from their home and be sure not to take them directly from the river due to various local laws in place and never take from any historical or protected site that may be nearby.
- **Animal companions:** statues and figurines of various animals all serve as evocative pieces to represent the

Goddess especially drawing upon the swan, sheep, salmon and boar.

- **Elemental symbols:** Blue is the colour of serenity, freedom and wisdom contained in the element of water. Colour has always held profound significance in spiritual practice with blue embodying energies related to water. Blue can be actively incorporated through an altar cloth, candles and crystals like blue lace agate, aquamarine, blue calcite etc. Personally, I do not use crystals for my own altar or practice but if you wish to do so, be sure they are sourced ethically and respectfully. You can also use Solar correspondences for the summer link within Sabrina's Welsh name, including pictures and items related to the sun.

- **Vessels:** Bowls, containers, bottles, chalices, and cauldrons can all be used to aid the storage of sacred water when working with Sabrina. With bottles and containers, it is essential to label them and that the water is frequently changed to avoid stagnant energy. In fact, the waters of the Goddess, whether collected from the River Severn or from another source in which she has been invoked into, should never be stored for too long. According to my local lore those who restricted Sabrina would know no peace due to the strength of her fists perpetually drumming upon the sides of the vessel that contained her.

Cleansing Spray

Rivers are perpetual motion in action; a natural phenomenon capable of breaking down anything within their path and disposing of it far away from its original placement. This is why rivers are heavily associated with acts of cleansing and purification as their energy helps to wash away anything unwanted. In the same way we cleanse our physical body, our surroundings also need to be decontaminated from the residual energy we have collected throughout the day. For our personal spaces, sprays are an easy and beginner friendly method to use while invoking the power of Sabrina.

You will need:

- An empty spray mist bottle, glass if possible
- Distilled water
- A preservative such as vodka or brandy
- Rosemary
- Juniper berries
- Orange rind
- Optional: essential oil of your choosing

Method:

- Pour distilled water into a saucepan.
- Before adding your other ingredients, hold the rosemary, juniper berries and orange rind individually and thank it for its assistance. Place these into the water and bring to the boil as well as adding in your preservative to stave off mould. You can also add a few drops of your chosen essential oil, no more than a couple will do.
- While the mixture steeps, place your hand over it so that you can feel its warmth rising and recite:

Sabrina
Great Goddess who protects and nourishes all who thrive
*   in your water*
I humbly ask for your blessings upon this mixture
And embrace your power to cleanse and purify
With your ever flowing river

- Strain the liquid into a spray bottle and use wherever you feel it necessary including individual rooms, around entrances, windowsills, or your tools. While you do this visualise Sabrina's river cleansing the space and protecting against anything that may be lingering.

Three Sisters Blessing

Blessings by water are prevalent throughout history. When we reflect on Sabrina's creation, especially the story of the three sisters, not only do we see the notion of triplicity inherent throughout Celtic cosmology, but we also witness the imparting of distinct gifts. Sabrina, the lover of people and culture shared her knowledge and shaped the land in accordance with her will so that it could thrive. Rheidol, with eagerness flowing through her body, was the first sister to establishing the connection between the rugged landscape and the sea with a mighty energy that can be felt within her waves. And Wye, in her slow and steady pace, gave tranquillity to the countryside to match her beauty. Sometimes we need that extra blessing to get us through the day and the Goddesses each possess a gift to see us through if we request it with an open heart

You will need:

- Three small bowls
- Water gathered from three different, natural sources
- Three Willow branches measuring 20cm each. Willow is sacred to all three goddesses due to its presence on their banks but if not obtainable three branches of your choosing will do.
- A piece of jewellery such as a necklace or ring
- Incense

- A fire-proof container
- Charcoal disk
- Lighter

Method:

- Whether its upon your altar or outside on the floor, construct an upside-down triangle using the three willow branches, with the apex facing towards you. This is the symbol for water within Western Alchemy but to me it is the perfect representation of the river journey from the mountains flowing down in one single point towards the sea.
- Position a bowl at each of the three corners and fill each one will spring water.
- In the centre of the triangle place your fireproof container. Then light your charcoal disk and place a small amount of incense upon it using the recipe in the Labyrinth exercise.
- If you can, sit comfortably or stand if you wish and close your eyes, breathe deeply and the incense fills the air with sweet aroma.
- Visualise the mighty Pumlumon, the stoic and time weathered giant. His eyes are glowing and tearful and with one blink he disperses three tears that cascade down his moss-covered face. Begin to recite:

I gaze upon Pumlumons eyes
Father of life from tears he cries
Bestower of the daughters, three
Who flow with bliss and mirth to me
Daughters of creation, imbued with power
I welcome your presence upon this hour

- As you hold the image in your mind, visualize the three tears begin to grow until they crash and flow into each of the three bowls upon the triangle, Rheidol to the right, Sabrina in front of you, and Wye to the left.
- Take your piece of jewellery and starting with Rheidol submerge it into the bowl and say in English or in Welsh:

Rheidol, Duwies fentrus
Merch gyflymaf Pumlumon
Bendithia fi i fod yn ddewr
Rheidol, Adventurous Goddess
Fastest daughter of Pumlumon
Bless me to be fearless

- Next take your jewellery and place it in the bowl in front of you containing Sabrina and say:

Hafren, Duwies y bobl
Merch ddoeth Pumlumon
Bendithia fi â gwybodaeth
Sabrina, Goddess of the people
Wisest daughter of Pumlumon
Bless me with Knowledge

- Finally take your jewellery and submerge it into the last bowl with Wye and say:

Gwy, Duwies amyneddgar
Merch hardd Pumlumon
Bendithia fi â llawenydd
Wye, Patient Goddess
Beautiful daughter of Pumlumon
Bless me with joy

- Place the jewellery upon your person and feel the gifts of fearlessness, wisdom and joy from the three sisters flow through your body.
- Thank each of the goddesses for their gift and afterwards combine all three bowls of water together so the sisters can be reunited. Take this outside to give back to the land so that they might be free once more.
- Make an offering and dispose of the incense.

Poppet Curse

The waters of Sabrina have known pain, disrespect and injustice and are no strangers to retaliation. When embarking upon our own journeys, it is likely we too will encounter events of this nature from those who do not have our best interests at heart or who actively wish harm against us. While a magical practice gifts us the ability to enact out change in accordance with our will with the help of our deities and spirits, it also supplies us with the means to attain justice.

Combined with aid from Sabrina who is heavily associated with protection, boundaries and equity, the effects of our magic can be potent. Witchcraft is inherently transgressive against the norms of a conformist society, wielded by the marginalised and downtrodden as a tool against the oppressive. Just like Sabrina's river who seeks the freedom of the wild ocean, balancing the cycles of life and death, so too does our craft harness both the beneficent and maleficent. Many may refrain from the idea of baneful magic in fear of a universal rebound effect. However, this concept is quite alien to the folk practices that originate in the land of Sabrina and was certainly never accepted by witches or cunning folk of the past. It seems to me a little too close to Christian morality, where every action is judged and assigned a moral value, stripping you of any means of empowerment.

I would never force someone to enact out a curse, nor would I promote a casual attitude towards cursing. I'm not going to curse John down the road just because his cat defecated in my garden, though I may launch it back with a shovel. Ethical considerations are a must with proper thought and reason why it should be conducted in the first place. But is there is one thing Sabrina has taught me in my practice, is that there are certain instances where we have been made to feel unsafe and vulnerable that require a curse. Just like any river in the natural world, they are no passive entities but are fully equipped with immense power to raise havoc. Therefore, I offer this spell to request aid against those who seek to abuse and cut us down, those who belittle, control and crush our spirit and will not disappear with blessings of love and light. Sabrina is beauty, passion, tranquillity but also rage, pain and anguish, all of which can be utilised for the benefit of our protection.

You will need:

- Water gathered from a river or other natural source
- A large bowl
- Clay to form a poppet
- Personal artifacts from the person the poppet represents. This can be hair, fingernails, a piece of fabric they own or if this is not available a photo of them with their name and date of birth written on it.

Method:

- With your clay begin to mould a poppet in the shape of the person you wish it to represent. While doing this place your personal artifact inside and visualise the person, what they look like, sound like and how they make you feel with their cruel behaviour. Feel that rage bubble up inside you.

- When the poppet has been formed, clasp it with both hands and envision a glowing red light. This is the life force, the living current that binds it to the person. Feel it pulsate with the rhythm of a heartbeat and as you do this say:

By my power I do decree
(Name of the person) this poppet shall be
Linked and connected by shape and design
Your life with this doll shall entwine

- Breathe on the poppet to infuse it with life and leave it to dry for a few hours so it's hard enough not to lose its shape but not too hard to the point it has completely set.
- Collect your water in your bowl and set upon a flat surface. With your hands hovering over, close your eyes and invoke Sabrina using the famous words of Milton which have echoed throughout time the Goddess' protective nature:

Sabrina fair,
Listen where thou art sitting
Under glassy, cool, translucent wave,
In twisted braids of lilies knitting,
The loose train of thy amber-dropping hair;
Listen for dear honour's sake,
Goddess of the silver lake,
Listen and save!

- Submerge the poppet underwater and begin to break each piece off in your hands starting with the feet and working your way up to the head. Visualise the persons influence over you breaking down, succumbing to the power of Sabrina's water. As you do this repeat these words:

Swirling with ravenous force
Water consumes upon its course
Your lies and hurt have now transpired
But shall sink down low, feeble, retired
I destroy your intent with Sabrina's aid
With this poppet in your image made
Bound within the rivers flow
Far from me you now shall go

- Ground yourself by breathing deeply and feeling your energy disperse into the ground and then dispose of the poppet remains into the nearest bin and throw the water on to a road away from any natural setting. They have no power over you now and any harm that have caused shall swiftly be wreaked upon them.
- Cleanse yourself in any way you see fit, whether that be through a calming bath, meditation or through the cleansing spray we made earlier.

Chapter 8

Serpents of the Deep

We are in an age of ecological decline. Destruction of habitats has forced various species to the brink of extinction. The increase in global temperature walks hand in hand with the profound threat towards all nature and life. And while greed, cruelty, and other incentives continue to exploit various territories, we are forced to witness Goddesses like Sabrina be poisoned, neglected, and disembodied from their divine status.

It is a scary time we are living in, especially when surrounded by the persistent knocking of consequence upon our front doors. Many people, me included, have felt hopeless and paralysed by both guilt and uncertainty towards the future of our planet when the news continues to report repeated incidents of ruination. We cannot turn a blind eye to this. The severity of our actions is staring us in the face with each one of us bearing some responsibility in the collective suffering experienced by nature as our society continues to adapt and grow. However, I write this chapter not to reprimand, or to add to that fear, nor to persuade you to quit all modern day undertaking and go live a feral life off grid where you are free to tend to the land and hunt out doc leaves for your toilet breaks. I write this as a message of hope and to initiate a conscious effort in restoring sovereign rule back to nature, specifically our rivers.

The fault is not ours alone, despite multiple companies pointing the finger at us under the notion of "serving our needs" while failing to acknowledge the devastation they have wrought in the name of economic success. We may feel powerless when we compare our efforts of recycling our household waste to the acceleration of industrialisation and the levels of pollution that comes with it. It is also increasingly difficult when our beliefs come into conflict with the materialistic culture of society. But without opposition to this our rivers will continue to bear no intrinsic value and serve as nothing more than a commodity. Without protection, we endanger all that is encompassed by the Goddess including our own wellbeing. To do this we need to significantly rethink our way of devotion to the deities and what it means to be in relation to Sabrina today.

Within Paganism and witchcraft, it can be easy to view deities as stagnant, but they do not stay the same. They are forever changing. Sabrina adopts the form that relates to the needs of the people who call to her, and these needs are ever-changing. We are living in an age drastically different to our ancestors and therefore we cannot hold Sabrina to outdated concepts. In my own personal practice, she is truly entwined within the awareness of environmentalism and to forge relationship with her we must follow suit. When we express sufficient wakefulness towards Sabrina's domain, no matter how small the act may be, we are ensuring the Goddess' preservation for future generations as well as facilitating respect and relationality, the core tenets of Pagan belief. This can be achieved when we stay informed.

The State of Our Rivers

According to the latest reports[1] none of the rivers flowing through England are in healthy condition. Many fail to meet the expectations set by the water framework directive and a similar picture is painted across the border by reports from Afonydd Cymru, who have their own concerns about the extent of the damage. News reports can also be overwhelming or unclear as to the true extent of the problem I have attempted to break down the main contributing factors to Sabrina's river, but I encourage others to do research in their own time; the results will shock you just as much as they did me.

- Agricultural sector – The biggest affliction to Sabrina's river arises from different types of pollution from agricultural operations including fertilisers like Nitrogen and Phosphates seeping into the river which speeds up the process of eutrophication.[2] This is the increased growth of algae blooms in the river which makes the quality of water both unsafe and hazardous to biodiversity. Other pollutants include pesticides, sediments from soil erosion that contain harmful chemicals and lastly, bacteria from animal faeces.
- Sewage – The systems designed to carry away our waste are failing due to outdated treatments plants and poor infrastructure especially during heavy rain fall. In the event of floods, the government has permitted the discharging of sewage into the river. However, this is not regulated which means water companies can take advantage and they have been doing this for quite some time with or without the presence of floods.
- Industrial and urban pollution – Additional pollutants are released into the river increasing Total Organic Carbon.
- Climate change which is part of a horrendous cycle, contributes to flooding and drought conditions from weather extremes.
- Littering and plastic which many of us have witnessed floating either on the river or resting by the banks, left by the lazy and the careless.

A Serpent's Warning

The separation between us and Sabrina, the inequity between human and nonhuman beings and the chaos wrought upon her river all have their origin within the shifts of political, economic, and spiritual thought.[3] Yet Sabrina is no passive agent amongst all of this. We have previously touched upon her retributive qualities but when we dive deeper into her folklore, we discover a vestige of defence equipped with teeth and claws. It is a memory that behaves mercilessly and reminds all that control over nature is an illusion and the more we push the more it will respond with an insatiable hunger for destruction. This is encapsulated in the image of the dragon.

Throughout history, dragons have been depicted as evil, malicious creatures of rage and appetite, devouring everything in sight as well as being associated with the adversary in Christian imagery. You only have to look at the book of revelation to see the connection between dragons, Satan and the end of the world. But the works of author and professor of anthropology, Veronica Strang, have illuminated dragons, otherwise referred to as serpents, as the original divine beings that represented all bodies of water across different cultures and belief.[4] Their serpentine form embodied the cultural understanding of water's role in both creation and destruction before they were radically transformed by anthropomorphism and later vilification through the Patriarchy, capitalism and environmental encroachment.[5]

This is not to say Sabrina once existed as a serpent being in the evolution of belief towards her river. The motif of the dragon slaying hero like St George were quintessential features of many tales in the country which developed in different manners not necessarily attached to environmental awareness or a primordial serpent once worshipped. Nevertheless, the use of dragons in the vicinity of her river can take on new meanings and relevance today by helping to reveal a way for sustainable engagement. These serpents of prodigious power can inspire us to look to the Goddess' water with more respect and reverence, with the dragon utilised as a metaphorical mediator between enchantment and decimation as well as a representative of the Goddess' power. After all, many of the dragon tales that linger across the River Severn often involve the local people at the hands of nature's vengeance.

According to *The Ancient and Present State of Gloucestershire,*[6] a ferocious dragon of enormous scale once travelled up the course of the River Severn and laid waste to the people, cattle, and land of Deerhurst. However, its rampage was soon ended by the local hero John Smith, who sneakily approached its lair while the dragon slept, basking away in the sun. Seizing the moment, with his trusty axe in hand, John courageously swung with all his might and with one blow, decapitated the dragon ending its reign of terror. For such bravery the King issued him an estate within the parish for him and his family to live upon for many years to come. A similar story also takes places just a few miles up north of Deerhurst in the hamlet of Coombe Hill.[7] In the same manner, a ravenous serpent of incredible size swam up the River Severn and nestled within its twists and curves, devouring the locals as it saw fit. However, a local man by the name of Tom Smith gained the creatures trust by feeding it roast pig. The serpent dropped its defences and consumed the delicacy that it had been presented with, which granted the perfect opportunity for Tom to strike with his axe. As a result of ridding the people of their terror, Tom was rewarded with an endless supply of beer.

Alongside the Somerset coast, overlooking the Bristol Cannel where Sabrina flows through to the sea, is the tale of another Dragon by the name of Blue Ben of Kilve.[8] According to lore, this fearsome creature was said to bathe in the waters to cool off before he was seized by the Devil to be his personal steed through the fires of hell. Blue Ben, unable to bear the heat from the fire, managed to escape the Devil but unfortunately became trapped and suffocated in the mudflats near his lair. What's interesting about the story of Blue Ben is that it specifically relates to the 19th century discovery of an Ichthyosaurus skull; a prehistoric marine reptile that once dominated the seas millions of years ago. Recently, another Ichthyosaur skeleton has been found near the Aust cliff which may have been the biggest of its kind, reaching up to an estimate of 20 to 25 meters long. This has since been dubbed the Ichthyotitan Severnensis or giant fish lizard of the River Severn. Perhaps the mythos of the dragon doesn't seem to far outlandish where the story itself connects the present with relics of the distant pass to produce an inspired fear towards the River Severn. If we do not act, the dragon of the River Severn may yet rise again, in the form of avoidable climate catastrophes.

The Path to Enchantment

To establish a deeper relationship with Sabrina is to recognise her intrinsic personhood. The earliest inhabitants of the River Severn's land knew her sentience, her idiosyncrasies expressed within each lapping wave and abided by her precious cycles. This sentiment has been hidden away by the forcefulness of disenchantment, but it is not entirely lost.

There remains a glimmer of hope echoing from within the visceral. The feelings of belonging, empathy, and the need to be free from any repressive shackle grows stronger everyday with each passing generation beckoned to observe the beauty and vitality of our blue home. More people are growing consciously aware that the world is filled with a multitude of beings or spirits, each one as autonomous as the next. Although some may not be tangible or easily perceived with the naked eye, each one has a unique identity as diverse as the land or culture they originate from. This is referred to as animism, the oldest of belief systems which allows us to understand the world we live in as inspirited and interconnected and can aid us in forming respectful relations.[9]

Acknowledging the Goddess' personhood is not just simply stating her presence exists simultaneously alongside our own, but it is the active removal of ourselves from the centre of importance, from a place of ego and domination of human experience. We exist in relation to the Goddess, never separate, and our actions must reflect this. Our practices must be centred on equity and entanglement with Sabrina's river where appreciation and respect intersect, allowing for our relationship to grow stronger with each passing devotion or action in honour of her name. By accomplishing this we are actively demonstrating effort to the Goddess who in return can strengthen our magic when we request her aid as well as help us to be a part of a living and vibrant world.

This isn't always the easiest path to tread when consumerism is deeply embedded. But the preachings of fear and relentless education are unlikely to orientate the hearts of the masses towards Sabrina on their own. Our answer to the Goddess' cry lies deep within, the numinous part of our existence that yearns for connection. The answer is awe. To be awe struck is to be enchanted by the mysteries of Sabrina and the River Severn. The inspiration to be found within her stories, the wonder of the memories, traditions and ancestry she contains and the qualities of her water itself all allow for the selfishness of individuality to be stripped away to pave the way for integration into a collective whole, a world of belonging, emotion and community. We can never fully eradicate the harmful things we do in the everyday world but through awe we can moderate and balance what we do with the conscious effort to be more respectful. Awe is the light that paves the way to Sabrina and creates the narrative that allows us to address the issues that face her river with a hunger for change that is driven through love and appreciation.

This has begun to be implemented through the combination of spirituality with the arts which conveys the powerful message of saving our rivers through enchantment and awe. For example, the River Wye, Sabrina's sister, has been undergoing a slow and painful deterioration with the status of the river regarded as "unfavourable-declining". However, from the depths, campaigners, artists, and environmental activists came together to create the Goddess Wye, a three-metre puppet to lead their parades and protests, to capture attention and to bring community together to represent why the river should be celebrated and urgently saved. Sabrina herself has also been made into a puppet of a similar vein, sporting a ship on her head, and can often been seen roaming the streets of Gloucester to enchant all who live by her to remember their connection to the glorious beauty of her river. Curiosity, intuition, heartfelt connection, and mystery pave the way for new visceral insight and change.

A New Pledge

The River Severn actively represents liberation. The Goddess seeks her way through the twisting curvatures of the land. She adapts, she modifies, and she is intricate in her movement. When we take note of her river and its role it plays in sustaining the land we too can act by changing, adapting and being liberated from repression and the harmful devastation of the modern age. We are water after all, connected in vast manners to the home of the Goddess.

Taking all of what I have covered in this chapter we can utilise this to carve a new way of devotion. I don't expect everyone to go to the extreme when it comes to her preservation. I would be a hypocrite if I did when I too am subject to the hustle of everyday life. But we can show our commitment to the relationship we forge with her through meaningful environmentally friendly acts that help aid the protection of her river. This includes:

1. **Reducing the use of plastic:** The waste from plastic alone is astronomical combined with the levels of chemical and pollutants during manufacturing. But reusable cups, bottles, lunch boxes, shopping bags, straws etc are all wonderful ways to reduce its usage. Day to day we are all subject to the busyness of life which necessitates plastic convenience especially when running to the shop to grab

quick drink. You shouldn't feel guilty about this every time, but balance and moderation are key; take the bottle with you to either recycle at the nearest bin or at home. Substitutes are also perfect for making sure the plastic impact is lessened on the river. For example, swapping cling film for reusable silicone dish covers to cover food.

2. **Biodegradable cleaning products:** This refers to the ingredients contained within which can effectively degrade entirely without causing damage to the environment. When we use our everyday cleaners, a vast majority of them end up down the drain, which eventually ends up polluting the river. There are some wonderful ecofriendly products out there on the market but so many recipes can be concocted at home. It's amazing what a bottle of white vinegar, bicarbonate soda and lemon juice can do.

3. **Litter picking:** what better way to actively demonstrate devotion to Sabrina than by helping to clean up her home. So much litter can be observed around river banks including plastic bottles, wrappers and crisp packets. However, you should always be careful when picking up litter, wear gloves and especially avoid glass, razor blades, etc (these are best dealt with by advising a local council member).

4. **Campaigning and volunteering:** Opportunities for big clean ups always present themselves, which can help restore the natural health of the river as well as for habitat renovation and water quality testing. Unfortunately, these may not be accessible for everyone due to personal circumstances but there are so many things that can be done at home regardless of proximity to Sabrina. For one, your voice is a powerful tool for the protection of the river and should never be silenced. Signing online petitions, campaigns and fundraising all help as well as

getting loud with the local representatives to demand for better care. Sometimes I feel guilty about the level of volunteering I can do as time restraints sometimes make it impossible. However, I have always said if you have a talent or skill, utilise it. As a devotion to Sabrina, I love to crochet and will often weave together beautiful creations to sell and raise funds to donate to causes that protect her.

5. **Less water usage:** You wouldn't think it at first but Sabrina's river, alongside many other rivers, face water scarcity both from natural occurring processes and from excessive consumption by water companies. This is then treated and used within our homes which will, more often than not, be wasted. We use water all the time without thinking about it, from daily showers, to washing and going to the toilet. But the less we use the less will be withdrawn from the river. This doesn't take a massive effort at all and the best thing about it is it will save your water bill; a win/win situation. Ways to achieve this includes spending less time in the shower or at least turning it off when you need to shave in between, turning the tap off when you brush your teeth, doing full load cycles on your washing machine.

6. **Enchantment:** Keep the memory of the Goddess alive. Tell her stories, spread awareness, and use them to inspire creative pieces so that a new generation can maintain a connection with Sabrina; this was the main reason I wrote this book. This recently happened in Newham-on-Severn with the River Severn sisters whereby a group of artists and story tellers united to create the most beautiful pieces inspired by the myths of the River Severn. There are also several places that keep the enchantment of the Goddess flowing including local Goddess Temples that have developed nearby the river including those situated in Stroud and Bristol.

Conclusion

From the heart of Wales, the mountain born Goddess spills from the fringes of her bog peat; yearning to fulfil her curiosity of the lands dwelling below. Coursing through the dramatic valleys, embraced by meadows and phantoms of former heroes, she finds solace in the quaint villages and towns of Powys, Shropshire and Worcestershire; to grow in wisdom, beauty and renown. The tranquillity of the countryside can only hold her impetuous nature for so long, for she hears the call of the salty shores beckoning her forth. With all her might, she flows through Gloucestershire to finally join with the rest of her sisters who await her arrival in the vast, open sea. There they travel to wherever their hearts please. This may be back to the mountain, this may be to the far and distant lands beyond, but the Goddess knows that wherever she goes, the voices of adoration and reverence will always follow.

We have explored and felt the presence of the Goddess Sabrina, revelling in each wave of mystery she washes over us. Sabrina is more than just a river but a multi-faceted entity who sits at the threshold between humanity and the Otherworld, watching all that has passed and all that will come. Her life-giving waters continue in their movement and wisdom, eagerly awaiting to take on new form to represent what Sabrina's people need them to be. But no matter how much she changes, or what form she takes, there is always one thing that stays the same. This is the feeling of liberation that comes when embracing her river. To step into it is to feel renewed and free as we dissolve into her presence, allowing ourselves in those moments of spiritual revelation to feel safe, knowing that we are cradled in her arms.

It is my hope that I have captured the magic and beauty of the Goddess who plays such a vital role in my life. Though her history may be overcast by academic unsurety, her energy is all encompassing upon the lands of the Marches, saturated in history, belief and culture, cultivated by years of interaction amongst the Sabrina Folk. I have tried to cover as much as possible including my own personal experiences, but with new discoveries each day and more and more people coming to the Goddess, who knows what else awaits those who invite Sabrina into their life. What new visions will she impart or what remnants of divinity will we uncover from the earth. In this vein, I hope that this book can give a solid foundation to understand and be inspired by her.

Sabrina defies containment, a ubiquitous Goddess that has stood the test of time in different appearances. She is the boundary that challenges homogeneity, who embraces the outcasts and defends against strife. She is the guardian of life, the parental source of love and the oncoming ruin of those who challenge her with desecration. But most importantly she is the elegance behind every ripple of water who waits patiently for her children to return to her.

And so, the next step is yours to take. I have offered suggestions and a snapshot of history to sink your teeth into and aid you in the process of connecting with her if you wish to do so. However, each and everyone's relationship with Sabrina will be different depending on how she calls to us. What's important is that her call is answered with an open heart and respectful thought especially regarding our interactions with the environment. Study her origins, leave offerings, talk to her regularly and flow with the Goddess on whatever journey she may take you. But always remember, she is listening, ready to answer the prayer of those who call out to her. Sabrina, Goddess of the silver lake, may you always listen and save!

End Notes

Introduction

1. Milton, J. (1876). *The mask of Comus*. JW Schermerhorn.
2. Dodd, M. S., Papineau, D., Grenne, T., Slack, J. F., Rittner, M., Pirajno, F., ... & Little, C. T. (2017). Evidence for early life in Earth's oldest hydrothermal vent precipitates. *Nature, 543*(7643), 60–64. https://doi.org/10.1038/nature21377
3. Rappenglueck, M. A. (2014). The cosmic deep blue: the significance of the celestial water world sphere across cultures. *Mediterranean Archaeology and Archaeometry, 14*(3), 293–305. Accessed February 20th 2024, https://www.maajournal.com/index.php/maa/article/view/906
4. Chumlea, W. C., Guo, S. S., Zeller, C. M., Reo, N. V., & Siervogel, R. M. (1999). Total body water data for white adults 18 to 64 years of age: the Fels Longitudinal Study. *Kidney international, 56*(1), 244–252. https://doi.org/10.1046/j.1523-1755.1999.00532.x
5. Lovelock, J., & Margulis, L. (2007). The Gaia Hypothesis. *New York*.
6. Nennius, F. (2018). *History of the Britons*. British American Books.

Chapter 1: Beloved Nymph

1. Armstrong, K. (2008). *A short history of myth*. Canongate Books.
2. May, R. (1991). *The cry for myth*. WW Norton & Company.
3. Hughes, K. (2014). *The Book of Celtic Magic: Transformative Teachings from the Cauldron of Awen*. Llewellyn Worldwide.
4. Thorpe, L. (2015). *The History of the Kings of Britain*. Penguin UK.
5. Henley, G. (2020). *A Companion to Geoffrey of Monmouth*. Brill, Leiden, Boston.

6. Rhys, J. (2020). *Celtic Folklore Welsh and Manx* (Vol. 1). Library of Alexandria.
7. Davies, J. C. (1911*). Folk-lore of West and Mid-Wales*. Printed at the "Welsh Gazette" Offices, 1911.
8. Booker, L. (1834) *The Springs of Plynlimmon*. Wolverhampton: printed by William Parke.

Chapter 2: A Historical Goddess

1. Ptolemaeus, C. (1991). The Geography, translated by EL Stevenson.
2. Fitzpatrick-Matthews, K. J. (2013). Britannia in the Ravenna Cosmography: a reassessment. Accessed February 25th 2024 https://www.academia.edu/4175080/BRITANNIA_IN_THE_RAVENNA_COSMOGRAPHY_A_REASSESSMENT
3. Hadas, M., Brodribb, W. J., Church, A. J., & Tacitus, C. (1942). *Complete Works of Tacitus: The Annals; The History; The Life of Cnaeus Julius Agricola; Germany and Its Tribes; A Dialogue on*. Random House.
4. Vol.74: Stream names of the River Severn Basin in Montgomeryshire (1986) Montgomeryshire collections relating to Montgomeryshire and its border, p68.
5. Bosworth, J. (1898). *An Anglo-Saxon Dictionary: Based on the Manuscript Collections of the Late Joseph Bosworth.* (Vol. 2). Clarendon Press.
6. Raithby, John, ed. (1819). Charles II, 1677 & 1678: An Act for Preservation of Fishing in the River of Seaverne. British History Online. pp. 892–893. Accessed 20th January 2024 https://www.british-history.ac.uk/statutes-realm/vol5/pp892–893.
7. Waters, B. (1947). *Severn Tide*. JM Dent.
8. Definition given by GPC Cymru.
9. Archaeologia Cambrensis, 1878. p328.
10. Archaeologia Cambrensis, 1937, p 27.

11. Bygones relating to Wales and the border counties, 1898, p 30.

12. Definition given by GPC Cymru.

13. Breeze, A. (2018) And thick on Severn snow the leaves. *The Housman Society Journal*, 44, 47–59. Accessed March 3rd 2024 https://www.housman-society.co.uk/wp-content/uploads/2018-housman-journal.pdf

14. Bygones relating to Wales and the border counties, 1873, p 6.

15. Eckwall, E. (1928). English River Names, Oxford: Clarendon Press.

16. O'Sullivan, A. (2007). Exploring past people's interactions with wetland environments in Ireland. *Proceedings of the Royal Irish Academy. Section C: Archaeology, Celtic Studies, History, Linguistics, Literature*, 147–203. https://doi.org/10.1353/ria.2007.0005

17. Bradley, R. (1990). *The passage of arms: an archaeological analysis of prehistoric hoards and votive deposits*. CUP Archive.

18. Hutton, R. (2013). *Pagan Britain*. Yale University Press.

19. York, J. 2002: The life cycle of Bronze Age metalwork from the River Thames. *Oxford Journal of Archaeology* **21**(1), 77–92 https://doi.org/10.1111/1468-0092.00150

20. Mullin, D. (2012). The river has never divided us: bronze Age metalwork deposition in western Britain. *Oxford journal of archaeology*, 31(1), 47–57. https://doi.org/10.1111/j.1468-0092.2011.00378.x

21. McCormack, B. (2006). *Monuments in The Landscape. Volume X1. Prehistoric Sites of Montgomeryshire*. Logaston Press.

22. Alcock, J. P. (2009). *Daily life of the pagan Celts*. Greenwood

23. Cunliffe, B. (2003). *The Celts: a very short introduction*. OUP Oxford.

24. Hutton, R. (2013). *Pagan Britain*. Yale University Press.

25. Yeates, S. J. (2008). *Tribe of witches: the religion of the" Dobunni" and" Hwicce"*. Oxbow Books.

26. Higgins, D.H. (2011). Aust (Gloucestershire) and Myths of Romes Second *Augusta* Legion and St Augustine's 'Oak' Conference. *Trans. Bristol & Gloucestershire Archaeological Society, 129.* 117–137. Accessed April 7th 2024 https://www.bgas.org.uk/tbgas_bg/v129/bg129117.pdf

27. Dames, M. (2019). *Spirts of Severn.* Austin Macauley Publishers Ltd.

28. Yeates, S. J. (2008). *Tribe of witches: the religion of the" Dobunni" and" Hwicce".* Oxbow Books.

29. Green, M. A. (2011). *The gods of the Celts.* The History Press.

30. Reynolds, L. (2022). *Roman rural settlement in Wales and the Marches: approaches to settlement and material culture through big data.* BAR Publishing.

31. Lee, S. (2015). Celtic Romanization: Cultural Assimilation or Cultural Exchange? *Young Historians Conference,* 6. Accessed April 12th 2024 https://pdxscholar.library.pdx.edu/younghistorians/2015/oralpres/6?utm_source=pdxscholar.library.pdx.edu%2Fyounghistorians%2F2015%2Foralpres%2F6&utm_medium=PDF&utm_campaign=PDFCoverPages

32. Webster, J. (2001). Creolizing the Roman provinces. *American journal of archaeology, 105*(2), 209–225. http://www.jstor.org/stable/507271

33. Aldhouse-Green, M. (2018). *Sacred Britannia: the gods and rituals of Roman Britain.* Thames & Hudson.

34. Larson, J. L. (2001). *Greek nymphs: Myth, cult, lore.* Oxford University Press, USA.

35. Macer-Wright, D. (2020). Temple of Sabrina A nymphaeum to the nymphs of the Springs. Temple of Sabrina A nymphaeum to the nymphs of the Springs – Littledean Roman Temple and Nymphaeum (wordpress.com).

36. Holbrook, N. (2006). the Roman period. *N. Holbrook and J. Juřica (eds),* 97–131. Accessed March 29th 2024 https://www.cotswoldarchaeology.co.uk/wp-content/

uploads/2014/11/Bristol-Gloucestershire-Archaeological-Report-No.-3r_part-3.pdf

37. RIB 306.
38. Trubshaw, B. (2015). *Dream incubation*. Avebury, UK: Heart of Albion.
39. Smith, K. (2005). *Domesticated dogs in the art and archaeology of iron age and Roman Britain*. University of South Wales (United Kingdom).
40. Tolkien, J. R. R. (2007). The Name" Nodens". *Tolkien Studies*, 4(1), 177–183. https://doi.org/10.1353/tks.2007.0032
41. Bromwich, R. (Ed.). (2014). *Trioedd Ynys Prydein: The Triads of the Island of Britain*. University of Wales Press.
42. Dames, M. (2019). *Spirts of Severn*. Austin Macauley Publishers Ltd.
43. Young, F. (2023). *Twilight of the Godlings: The Shadowy Beginnings of Britain's Supernatural Beings*. Cambridge University Press.
44. Hutton, R. (2011). How pagan were medieval English peasants? *Folklore, 122*(3), 235–249. https://doi.org/10.1080/0015587X.2011.608262
45. Bromwich, R. (Ed.). (2014). *Trioedd Ynys Prydein: The Triads of the Island of Britain*. University of Wales Press.

Chapter 3: The Poet's Eternal Muse

1. Kaufman, E. 'Of Albions glorious Ile the Wonders… I write'. How important is the land in early modern depictions of national identity? INNERVATE Leading Undergraduate Work in English Studies, Volume 3 (2010–2011), pp. 178–192.
2. Hayman, R. (2012). *Severn*. Hereford: Logaston Press; First Edition.
3. Abram, D. (2017). The spell of the sensuous. *CSPA Quarterly*, (17), 22–24.
4. Hughes, K. (2021). *Cerridwen: Celtic Goddess of Inspiration*. Llewellyn Worldwide. p 207.

5. Olson, K. (2008). Gwendolyn and Estrildis: Invading Queen in British Historiography. In *Medieval Feminist Forum: A Journal of Gender and Sexuality* (Vol. 44, No. 1, pp. 36–52). Society for Medieval Feminist Scholarship. Accessed February 15th 2024 https://scholarworks.wmich.edu/mff/vol44/iss1/4/

6. Ellis, J. (2000). Embodying Dislocation: A Mirror for Magistrates and Property Relations. *Renaissance Quarterly*, 53(4), 1032–1053. doi:10.2307/2901455

7. Baldwin, W., Blenerhasset, T., Higgins, J., & Niccols, R. (1815). *Mirror for magistrates: in five parts* (Vol. 1). Lackington, Allen, and Company. p 74.

8. Murphy, E. (2011). Sabrina and the making of English history in Poly-Olbion and A Maske Presented at Ludlow Castle. *Studies in English Literature, 1500–1900*, 87–110. https://doi.org/10.1353/sel.2011.0001

9. Ibid

10. Shakespeare, W. (1734). *The Tragedy of Locrine, the eldest son of King Brutus*. J. Tonson, and the rest of the proprietors; and sold. URL: The Tragedy of Locrine: The Eldest Son of King Brutus – Wentworth Smith, William Shakespeare, Charles Tilney – Google Books.

11. Jones, A. L. (2013). *Darogan: Prophecy, lament and absent heroes in medieval Welsh literature*. University of Wales Press.

12. Kaufman, E. 'Of Albions glorious Ile the Wonders… I write'. How important is the land in early modern depictions of national identity? INNERVATE Leading Undergraduate Work in English Studies, Volume 3 (2010–2011), pp. 178–192.

13. Choi, E. (2009). The Court, the Rule, and the Queen: The Faerie Queene as a Representation of Elizabeth I. 영학논집 *(English Studies)*, 29, 196–210. Accessed March 11th 2024 https://hdl.handle.net/10371/2394

14. Parker, W. (2005). *The Four Branches of the Mabinogi*. Bardic Press. p 189.

15. Slaven, A. N. (2019). *Wilds and Wastes: How Wilderness Shaped Narratives of English National Identity in Spenser and Shakespeare*. University of Louisiana at Lafayette.

16. Barrett, C. (2018). Time River Body: Personification and Inappropriate Detail in Drayton's Poly-Olbion. Early Modern English Literature and the Poetics of Cartographic Anxiety. P89–135. Oxford University Press. https://doi.org/10.1093/oso/9780198816874.003.0003

17. Drayton, M. (1970). *Poly-olbion. Or A Chorographicall Description of Tracts, Rivers, Mountaines, Forests, and other Parts of this renowned Isle of Great Britaine, With intermixture of the most Remarquable Stories, Antiquities, Rarityes, Pleasures, and Commodities of the same: Digested in a Poem by Michael Drayton Esq. With a Table added, etc. [With the "Illustrations" of John Selden.]*. HL. P p 76.

18. Trevisan, S. (2010). MICHAEL DRAYTON'S'POLY-OLBION': A STUDY IN PERSPECTIVE. https://hdl.handle.net/11577/3426559

19. Drayton, M. (1970). *Poly-olbion. Or A Chorographicall Description of Tracts, Rivers, Mountaines, Forests, and other Parts of this renowned Isle of Great Britaine, With intermixture of the most Remarquable Stories, Antiquities, Rarityes, Pleasures, and Commodities of the same: Digested in a Poem by Michael Drayton Esq. With a Table added, etc. [With the "Illustrations" of John Selden.]*. HL. p 77.

20. Kaufman, E. 'Of Albions glorious Ile the Wonders... I write'. How important is the land in early modern depictions of national identity? INNERVATE Leading Undergraduate Work in English Studies, Volume 3 (2010–2011), pp. 178–192.

21. Milton, J. (1876). *The mask of Comus*. JW Schermerhorn. p 275.

Chapter 4: Bridge to the Otherworld

1. Beck, N. (2015). The River-Goddess in Celtic Traditions: Mother, Healer and Wisdom Purveyor. *Mélanges en l'honneur de Pierre-Yves Lambert.* hal-03275671

2. Rudiger, A. (2022). *Y Tylwyth Teg. an Analysis of a Literary Motif.* Bangor University (United Kingdom). Accessed June 2nd 2024 https://research.bangor.ac.uk/portal/en/theses/y-tylwyth-teg-an-analysis-of-a-literary-motif(619cf901-ff1d-4ecb-a74e-56a7e3491f0a).html

3. Williams, I. (Ed.). (1930). *Pedeir keinc y Mabinogi.* Gwasg Prifysgol Cymru.

4. Starling, M. (2022). *Welsh Witchcraft: A Guide to the Spirits, Lore and Magic of Wales.* Llewellyn Worldwide.

5. Rudiger, A. (2022). *Y Tylwyth Teg. an Analysis of a Literary Motif.* Bangor University (United Kingdom). Accessed June 2nd 2024 https://research.bangor.ac.uk/portal/en/theses/y-tylwyth-teg-an-analysis-of-a-literary-motif(619cf901-ff1d-4ecb-a74e-56a7e3491f0a).html

6. Starling, M. (2022). *Welsh Witchcraft: A Guide to the Spirits, Lore and Magic of Wales.* Llewellyn Worldwide.

7. Hughes, K. (2021). *Cerridwen: Celtic Goddess of Inspiration.* Llewellyn Worldwide.

8. Owen, E. (2019). *Welsh Folk-Lore a Collection of the Folk-Tales and Legends of North Wales.* Good Press.

9. Jones, E. (1813). *A Relation of Apparitions of Spirits in the County of Monmouth, and the Principality of Wales, Etc.* E. Lewis.

10. Bradley, A. G. (1920). *A Book of the River Severn.* London: Methuen & Co.

11. Rudiger, A. (2022). *Y Tylwyth Teg. an Analysis of a Literary Motif.* Bangor University (United Kingdom). Accessed June 2nd 2024 https://research.bangor.ac.uk/portal/en/theses/y-tylwyth-teg-an-analysis-of-a-literary-motif(619cf901-ff1d-4ecb-a74e-56a7e3491f0a).html

12. Trevelyan, M. (1909). *Folk-lore and Folk-stories of Wales.* E. Stock.

13. Suggett, R. (2008). *A history of magic and witchcraft in Wales.* History Press.

14. Ibid

15. Briggs, K. (1965). *Folk Tales of England.* Routledge and Kegan Paul PLC.

16. Tongue, R. L. (1970). *Forgotten folk-tales of the English counties.* Routledge & Kegan Paul Books.

17. Davies, S. (Ed.). (2007). *The Mabinogion.* Oxford University Press, USA.

18. Hunt, A. (2018, January 4). The Lydney Park Temple of Nodens as 'Avalon'. *Shadows in the Mist: The Quest for a Historical King Arthur.* Shadows in the Mist: The Quest for a Historical King Arthur: The Lydney Park Temple of Nodens as 'Avalon' (mistshadows.blogspot.com).

19. Davies, S. (Ed.). (2007). *The Mabinogion.* Oxford University Press, USA.

20. Telyndru, J. (2023). *The Ninefold Way of Avalon: Walking the Path of the Priestess.* Llewellyn Worldwide.

Chapter 5: The Sabrina Folk

1. Jackson, G. F. (1879). *Shropshire Word-Book, a Glossary of Archaic and Provincial Words, Etc., Used in the County; by Georgina F. Jackson.* Trübner & Company. p 871.

2. Bryden, D. J. (1981). The Iron Bridge, Symbol of the Industrial Revolution.

3. Hayman, R. (2012). *Severn.* Hereford: Logaston Press; First Edition.

4. Trinder, B. S. (2005). *Barges & Bargemen: A Social History of the Upper Severn Navigation 1660–1900.* Phillimore.

5. Randall, J. (1879*). Broseley and its Surroundings. A History.* The Salopian and West-Midland Journal. Available at:

https://www.broseley.org.uk/journal/broseley%20&%20
its%20surroundings.pdf

6.   Trinder, B. S. (2005). *Barges & Bargemen: A Social History of
     the Upper Severn Navigation 1660–1900*. Phillimore.

7.   Hayman, R. (2012). *Severn*. Hereford: Logaston Press; First
     Edition.

8.   Hornell, J. (1936). British coracles. *The Mariner's Mirror*,
     22(1), 5–41. https://doi.org/10.1080/00253359.1936.10657170

9.   Powell, J. (2009). *Ironbridge Gorge Through Time*. Amberley
     Publishing Limited.

10. Thornley, I. D. (1924). The destruction of sanctuary. *Tudor
     Studies*, 182–207.

11. Rees, E. A. (2001). *Welsh Outlaws and Bandits: Political
     Rebellion and Lawlessness in Wales, 1440–1603*.

12. Suggett, R. (2008). *A history of magic and witchcraft in Wales*.
     History Press.

13. Palmer, R. (1992). *The Folklore of Hereford & Worcester*.
     Logaston Press

14. Schwyzer, P. (1997). Purity and Danger on the West Bank
     of the River Severn: The Cultural Geography of A Masque
     Presented at Ludlow Castle, 1634. *Representations*, (60),
     22–48. https://doi.org/10.2307/2928804

15. Hayman, R. (2012). *Severn*. Hereford: Logaston Press; First
     Edition.

16. Palmer, R. (1992). *The Folklore of Hereford & Worcester*.
     Logaston Press.

17. Dames, M. (2019). *Spirts of Severn*. Austin Macauley
     Publishers Ltd.

18. Burne, C. S. (1883). *Shropshire folk-lore: a sheaf of gleanings*.
     Trübner.

19. Owen, E. (2019). *Welsh Folk-Lore a Collection of the Folk-Tales
     and Legends of North Wales*. Good Press.

20. Palmer, R. (1992). *The Folklore of Hereford & Worcester*.
     Logaston Press.

21. Scott-Davies, A. (2009). *Haunted Shropshire*. The History Press.

22. Shoop, M. P (1910). *Sabrina: The Class Goddess of Amherst College, a History*. Loring-Axtell Company.

23. Ibid

Chapter 6: Sacred Animals

1. Ross, A. (1993). *Pagan Celtic Britain: studies in iconography and tradition*. Constable.

2. Bygones relating to Wales and the border counties, 1872, p 7.

3. Owen, E. (2019). *Welsh Folk-Lore a Collection of the Folk-Tales and Legends of North Wales*. Good Press.

4. Gaskell, L. C.M. (1914). *Friends around the Wrekin*. London: Smith, Elder.

5. Potts, G. W., & Swaby, S. E. (1993). The fishes of the River Severn Estuary. *Available at: publications*, *18*(2018), 570.

6. Jenkins, J. G. (1972). The customs of Welsh fishermen. *Folklore*, *83*(1), 1–19. https://doi.org/10.1080/001558 7X.1972.9716451

7. Plec, E., Hughes, H., & Stalley, J. (2017). The salmon imperative. *Rhetoric Society Quarterly*, *47*(3), 247–256. https://doi.org/10.1080/02773945.2017.1309909

8. Burema, J. (2023). *The Salmon of Knowledge in Irish Literature; a Scholarly Concept* (Master's thesis). Accessed May 25th 2024 https://studenttheses.uu.nl/handle/20.500.12932/45567

9. Davies, S. (Ed.). (2007). *The Mabinogion*. Oxford University Press, USA.

10. Bromwich, R. (Ed.). (2014). *Trioedd Ynys Prydein: The Triads of the Island of Britain*. University of Wales Press.

11. Davies, S. (Ed.). (2007). *The Mabinogion*. Oxford University Press, USA. pp204–205

12. Evans, A. J., Nettleship, J., & Perry, S. (2008). Linn Liuan/ Llyn Llyw: The Wondrous Lake of the Historia Brittonum's

de Mirabilibus Britanniae and Culhwch ac Olwen. *Folklore,* *119*(3), 295–318. https://doi.org/10.1080/00155870802352236

13. Ibid

14. Bromwich, R., & Evans, D.S. (1988) Culhwch ac Olwen. Cardiff: University of Wales Press.

15. Aldhouse-Green, M. (2023). *Enchanted Wales: myth and magic in Welsh storytelling.* University of Wales Press.

16. Green, M. A. (2011). *The gods of the Celts.* The History Press.

17. Burne, C. S. (1883). *Shropshire folk-lore: a sheaf of gleanings.* Trübner.

18. *Garlick, S. F. (2011). Horses, swine and magical birds: The role of animals in the Mabinogion. University of Wales Trinity Saint David (United Kingdom).*

19. Bromwich, R. (Ed.). (2014). *Trioedd Ynys Prydein: The Triads of the Island of Britain.* University of Wales Press.p50.

20. Davies, S. (Ed.). (2007). *The Mabinogion.* Oxford University Press, USA.

21. Morus-Baird, G., (2023) *Taliesin Origins.* Celtic Source.

22. Munro, J. H. (2003). Medieval Woollens: Textiles, Textile Technology, and Industrial Organisation, c. 800–1500. *The Cambridge history of western textiles,* 2, 181–227.

23. Goodridge, J. (1990). *Rural life in English poetry of the mid-eighteenth century.* Nottingham Trent University (United Kingdom).

24. Dyer, J. (1757). *The Fleece: A Poem. In Four Books* (No. 17). R. and J. Dodsley.

Chapter 8: Serpents of the Deep

1. Rivers Trust, (2024, February). *State of our rivers Report.* Accessed March 19th 2024 *https://theriverstrust.org/rivers-report-2024*

2. Holden, J., Haygarth, P. M., Dunn, N., Harris, J., Harris, R. C., Humble, A., ... & Benton, T. (2017). Water quality and UK agriculture: challenges and opportunities. *Wiley*

Interdisciplinary Reviews: Water, 4(2), e1201. https://doi.
org/10.1002/wat2.1201

3.   Shaw, S., & Francis, A. (2014). *Deep blue: critical reflections on nature, religion and water*. Routledge.

4.   Strang, V. (2023). *Water beings: from nature worship to the environmental crisis*. Reaktion Books.

5.   Strang, V. (2014). Lording It over the Goddess: Water, gender, and human-environmental relations. *Journal of Feminist Studies in Religion*, 30(1), 85–109. https://doi. org/10.2979/jfemistudreli.30.1.85

6.   Atkyns, R. (1712). The ancient and present state of Glocestershire. https://archive.org/details/bim_ eighteenth-century_the-ancient-and-present-_atkyns-robert-sir_1712/page/551/mode/2up

7.   Brooks, R. (2010). *A Grim Almanac of Gloucestershire*. The History Press Ltd.

8.   Brewer, D. (2019). *Dragon Legends of Olde England*. Lulu. com.

9.   Harvey, G. (2017). *Animism: Respecting The Living World*. C Hurst 7 Co Publishers Ltd.

Bestsellers from Moon Books

Keeping Her Keys
An Introduction to Hekate's Modern Witchcraft
Cyndi Brannen
Blending Hekate, witchcraft and personal development
together to create a powerful new magickal perspective.
Paperback: 978-1-78904-075-3 ebook 978-1-78904-076-0

Journey to the Dark Goddess
How to Return to Your Soul
Jane Meredith
Discover the powerful secrets of the Dark Goddess and
transform your depression, grief and pain into healing
and integration.
Paperback: 978-1-84694-677-6 ebook: 978-1-78099-223-5

Shamanic Reiki
Expanded Ways of Working with Universal Life Force Energy
Llyn Roberts, Robert Levy
Shamanism and Reiki are each powerful ways of healing; together,
their power multiplies. Shamanic Reiki introduces techniques to
help healers and Reiki practitioners tap ancient healing wisdom.
Paperback: 978-1-84694-037-8 ebook: 978-1-84694-650-9

Southern Cunning
Folkloric Witchcraft in the American South
Aaron Oberon
Modern witchcraft with a Southern flair, this book is a
journey through the folklore of the American South and
a look at the power these stories hold for modern witches.
Paperback: 978-1-78904-196-5 ebook: 978-1-78904-197-2

Readers of ebooks can buy or view any of these bestsellers by clicking on the live link in the title. Most titles are published in paperback and as an ebook. Paperbacks are available in traditional bookshops. Both print and ebook formats are available online.

Find more titles and sign up to our readers' newsletter www.collectiveinkbooks.com/paganism

For video content, author interviews and more, please subscribe to our YouTube channel.

MoonBooksPublishing

Follow us on social media for book news, promotions and more:

Facebook: Moon Books

Instagram: @MoonBooksCI

X: @MoonBooksCI

TikTok: @MoonBooksCI